four basic practices

four basic practices

VEDANTA'S SĀDHANA-CATUṢṬAYA

SWAMI TYAGANANDA

First Edition: June 2025

ISBN: 978-0-9987314-6-9

contents

preface

What the late Joseph Dwyer said to me more than 25 years ago is still fresh in my mind. Joe was a longtime Vedānta student in his 60s, and I was in my 40s when I first met him. I had just arrived from India and Joe was my informal driving instructor. He was a kind, generous and patient teacher. He told me one day, "Swami, after the first snow every winter, I take my car to the parking lot of the mall near my home and practice driving on the snow." He said that although he had driven cars for decades under all conditions, he still felt it important to go back to the basics every winter to freshen up his muscle memory.

That struck a chord. *Going back to the basics!* Every one of us needs to do this now and then. The circumstances and the contexts may be different for everyone, but it is undeniable that changes do occur over time in the way we think and the way we do certain things. Change is natural and inevitable. So long as it doesn't take us away from the basics, we are safe. Oftentimes the changes are so subtle that we may not even notice them occurring in real time. An occasional "going back to the basics" plan can provide the assurance that we are on the right track. If we find that something isn't as it should be, it gives us a chance to work on improving it. That increases the chances of success.

How does a Vedānta student go back to the basics? One way to do that is to revisit the core practices of Vedānta. Traditionally, these are called "Four Practices" (*sādhana-catuṣṭaya*). What these four practices are, why they are the "basic" practices, what role they play in a Vedānta student's life, and how they lead ultimately to spiritual freedom—that is what this little book is about.

While Vedānta's Four Basic Practices are the heart of this book, it is helpful to begin by asking an even more basic question: What *is* Vedānta? The literal meaning of Vedānta, "the essence of the Vedas," is clear enough, but over time the word has come to mean many things to many people. The first chapter examines these different meanings and how they affect how we understand the world and our position in it.

An equally important question is regarding fitness to study Vedānta and to practice it. Vedānta's basic practices play an important role in determining both the fitness of the student and the pace of progress. This is addressed in chapter two. The Four Basic Practices then take up the bulk of the book—what each practice means, what challenges it presents, how the practice nourishes us, and how we can incorporate it in our daily lives.

Yoga is nothing but the Four Basic Practices in action. A chapter provides Vedānta's understanding of yoga. The purpose of yoga is to lead us to spiritual freedom. What this journey entails and what stages it passes through is discussed in another chapter. We discover that, when practiced sincerely and vigorously, the Four Basic Practices no longer appear to be "four," they become one with our life. No longer are they simply what we *do* but become a measure of who we truly *are*.

Most citations in the book are incorporated in the main text. The endnotes carry a few additional references and quotes for a deeper study. Not surprisingly, most references point to the Upaniṣads and the Gītā, but even more prolifically to the *Complete Works of Swami Vivekananda*. It is these nine volumes, which contain Swamiji's talks, writings, letters and conversations, that fired my interest in Vedānta from my teenage years, providing both inspiration and education, and launching me on a lifelong quest. It is to Swamiji that I owe everything.

Looking back I can now see how I unconsciously absorbed from my parents the essentials of spiritual living. Their quiet lives have left a deep mark on my mind. The swamis of the Ramakrishna Order have taught me enormously over the years, often in informal settings, through their guidance, conversations, and friendship. The study of Vedānta's Sanskrit texts under the guidance of Sri V. R. Kalyanasundara Sastrigal (1911-99) for many years in Chennai helped bring clarity to intricate issues. What little I know of Vedānta is due to these opportunities that came my way, and for that I am forever grateful. My heartfelt gratitude to Pravrajika Vrajaprana, of the Vedanta Society of Southern California in Santa Barbara, for her careful reading of the manuscript and insightful suggestions.

A book about spiritual practice should ideally be an inspiration to begin or to double down on practice. Books are important but are never enough to begin a definitive spiritual practice. It is possible to receive a practice specifically suited for us with the help of an authentic and experienced teacher. Perhaps many of us already have a practice of our own.

My hope is that after reading this book, or perhaps even in the midst of the reading, we will try to start practicing as best we can. Our "best" will keep getting better with time if we stick to the practice with sincerity and dedication, and not slacken our efforts. As Swami Vivekananda often said, "Arise! Awake! And stop not till the goal is reached."

Boston, June 2025

CHAPTER 1

recalibrating vedānta

What is Vedānta?—this question isn't uncommon in the West. But those who have even a nodding acquaintance with Eastern philosophical thought have heard about Vedānta. So what does the word mean to them? It's not an easy question to answer, because Vedānta has come to mean many things to many people.

Words are like living organisms. They evolve over time. Their meanings expand or contract in response to societal and cultural changes and expectations. That is what has happened to "Vedānta" as well. Its literal meaning is clear enough: Vedānta is a combination of two terms, Veda and *anta* ("essence" or "end"), meaning the essence of the Vedas or the end of the Vedas.

The Vedas are the preeminent Hindu scriptures which are believed to have no human author.[1] It is believed that the Vedas were revealed to seekers of Truth in deep meditations. These seekers are regarded as sages and seers of the Vedic revelations, not as authors of the Vedas. The revelations were transmitted and preserved orally and, when writing became the norm, were written on parchment. At some point in history, the great sage Vyāsa undertook the task of collecting these texts and compiling them into what became four books—Ṛg-veda, Yajur-veda, Sāma-veda, and Atharva-veda.

Each of these four books is divided into four parts. The first, called Saṁhitā, contains hymns and prayers; the second, called Brāhmaṇa, contains details regarding Vedic rituals and sacrifices; the third, called Āraṇyaka, contains various kinds of meditations; and the last, called Upaniṣad, contains the spiritual revelations that place the entire human experience into context, pointing out the real nature of the Self, its mysterious predicament, and the way to its eventual freedom (*mokṣa*).

The first three parts of the Vedas deal primarily with rituals, external and internal, and collectively form the "ritual section" (*karma-kāṇḍa*). The last part, which contains the Upaniṣads, deals with philosophy and forms the "knowledge section" (*jñāna-kāṇḍa*) of the Vedas. This section usually comes towards the end (*anta*) of each Veda and contains the principles and insights that tie together the wisdom found throughout the Vedas. The Upaniṣads thus embody the essence (*anta*) of the entire Vedas. As text, therefore, Vedānta primarily refers to the Upaniṣads.

The Upaniṣads often look like fragmentary notes, and it's not easy to discover the narrative that links the brilliant insights and truths scattered throughout those texts.[2] For that we turn to the commentaries written by great mystics and teachers who were able to discover the subtle links in these ancient texts and explain them. Not surprisingly, we see in these commentaries a range of interpretations, especially about the relationship between the embodied self (*jīvātman*) and the supreme self (*paramātman*). Those who hold that the two are distinct and forever separate belong to the dualistic school (*dvaita*). Those who hold that the two are related—the embodied self being a part of the supreme self—belong to the qualified nondualistic school (*viśiṣṭādvaita*). Those who hold that the two may *appear* as two but are really one and the same belong to the nondualistic school (*advaita*).

There have been many great interpreters throughout history and it is assumed that there will be more to come in the future. Some names stand out—such as Śrī Śaṅkarācārya (788–820) among the nondualists, Śrī Rāmānujācārya (1017–1137) among the qualified nondualists, and Śrī Madhvācārya (1238–1317) among the dualists. In their commentaries, these teachers present concise narratives that support their views and refute those of others. To bolster their arguments the teachers provide references not only from the Vedas but also from post-Vedic texts, mythology and history. The vital contribution of Swami Vivekananda (1863–1902) helps us to think of the different interpretations in evolutionary terms. As we evolve, our conceptual frameworks evolve as well. Every interpretation of these great teachers fulfills a need and, in one way or another, opens the door to the ultimate reality.

Among these teachers, the nondualists tend to depend almost exclusively on the Upaniṣads while others rely more on later texts. That is why the Upaniṣads have—at least in the popular mind—become identified with the nondualistic approach. Śrī Śaṅkarācārya's powerful influence on Indian philosophy also plays a significant role in identifying the Upaniṣads with nondualism. Therefore, to many people Vedānta seems inseparable from nondualistic thinking. The meaning of Vedānta thus becomes narrowed to a specific school of Indian philosophy.

As with other world religions which have been around for centuries, Hinduism is not a monolith. It is divided into sects, each with its own central deity, scripture, rituals, mythology, and traditions. Among the major sects in Hinduism are Śaiva (worshipers of Śiva), Vaiṣṇava (worshipers of Viṣṇu as Kṛṣṇa, Rāma, or Nārāyaṇa), and Śākta (worshipers of Kālī or other forms of the Divine Mother). Some tend to think of Vedānta as yet another sect, comprising "worshipers" of the Impersonal God.[3] Identifying Vedānta as one among the many Hindu sects is another way through which Vedānta's meaning becomes narrowed.

Each of these sects and sub-sects in Hinduism is in many ways radically different from other sects. What is astonishing is that, despite the staggering diversity, all these sects think of themselves as Hindu. What is it that connects them and gives them a shared identity? Adding to the complexity is the simple fact that no Hindu scripture has the word "Hindu" in it. These words—Hindu, Hinduism—are of a relatively recent origin. The sects and their followers have always seen themselves as a part of the "eternal way of life" (*sanātana dharma*). However they may have seen themselves in the past, today their self-identity as Hindu is firmly entrenched.

Among the things that all the sects of Hinduism share in common is the acknowledgment that the Vedas are the supreme authority.[4] While every Hindu sect usually has its own favored scripture other than the Vedas, all of them have the highest regard for the Vedas. They believe that, directly or indirectly, they have inherited the Vedic heritage and it is reflected in various ways through the life and practices of their people. Since Vedānta is, literally, the essence of the Vedas, it is possible to say that Vedānta provides the philosophical foundation on which the various Hindu sects have built their vast edifices. This way of thinking sees Vedānta as the underlying essence of what is recognized as Hinduism.

We have seen how Vedānta's meaning expands or contracts depending on how people perceive it. Vedānta's literal meaning is simply "the essence of the Vedas." As text, Vedānta is understood to be the Upaniṣads. As philosophy, Vedānta is often identified with nondualism. It is sometimes thought of as a sect or a tradition within Hinduism on par with sects such as Vaiṣṇava, Śaiva or Śākta. Many see Vedānta as the philosophical essence that provides the foundation to the multifarious ways in which Hinduism manifests in the world. All of these different perceptions of Vedānta revolve around the Vedas, which are generally thought of as the ancient and supreme books of Hinduism.

The idea that the Vedas are *books* is questionable, especially when we remember that the Vedas are considered to be without beginning and without end. Speaking at the Parliament of Religions in Chicago in 1893, Swami Vivekananda said:

> It may sound ludicrous to this audience, how a book can be without beginning or end. But by the Vedas no books are meant. They mean the accumulated treasury of spiritual laws discovered by different persons in different times. Just as the law of gravitation existed before its discovery, and would exist if all humanity forgot it, so is it with the laws that govern the spiritual world. The moral, ethical, and spiritual relations between soul and soul and between individual spirits and the Father of all spirits, were there before their discovery, and would remain even if we forgot them. (CW I. 6-7)

Whatever is true and real stands on its own authority and is independent of time, place and people. No country, no religion, no time in history, no place on earth can lay claim to the ownership of truth and reality.

Derived from the Sanskrit root *vid,* "to know," the word "Veda" primarily means knowledge. Vedānta therefore can as well be understood to be "the essence of knowledge." How can this be limited in any way and by anyone? God's revelations are eternal and unbounded. Speaking at Pasadena in California on January 28, 1900, Vivekananda said:

> Is God's book finished? Or is it still a continuous revelation going on? It is a marvelous book—these spiritual revelations of the world. The Bible, the Vedas, the Koran, and all other sacred books are but so many pages, and an infinite number of pages remain yet to be unfolded. I would leave it open for all of them. We stand in the present, but open ourselves to the infinite future. We take in all that has been in the past, enjoy the light of the present, and open every window of the heart for all that will come in the future. (CW 2. 374)

This insight frees Vedānta from every factor that tends to limit it to a specific book, or a specific school of philosophy, or a specific sect, or a specific religion. It identifies Vedānta with spirituality itself, which is truth without any frontiers. Even while acknowledging and embracing rituals and personalities, theologies and traditions, Vedānta transcends all these without denying them. Knowledge has no specific name, so even the word "Vedānta" disappears in the infinite effulgence of the divine presence.

There are no right or wrong answers here. Every way in which Vedānta is perceived serves a purpose and is useful as far as it goes. How students of Vedānta understand Vedānta shapes how they see themselves, how they see the world, and how they relate to others.

CHAPTER 2

spiritual fitness

Indra, the leader of the celestial beings, and Virocana, the leader of the demons, once approached Prajāpati. They were immediately told to spend thirty-two years practicing the disciplines of a celibate student. Only after that did Prajāpati ask them the purpose of their visit. When they told him of their desire to know the Ātman, he gave them a preliminary teaching.

The teaching satisfied Virocana. He felt that it was all he needed. He felt no need to explore and examine what was told because it seemed to confirm his own prior understanding, which was sadly superficial. Virocana thought of himself in terms of his body and, as he heard from Prajāpati, the Ātman was the self. Presto!—the body is the Ātman. Problem solved.

But the more Indra reflected on the teaching, the more questions arose in his heart. How could the perishable body be the imperishable self? He went back for clarification. Prajāpati made Indra undergo more moral and physical disciplines for another thirty-two years, at the end of which he imparted to Indra a deeper teaching on the Ātman. Indra was again assailed by doubts and he returned to Prajāpati to get his doubts resolved. Indra had to undergo similar disciplines for another thirty-two years before receiving a yet higher teaching.

When Indra's heart was still not satisfied and craved for greater clarity, he was made to stay and practice disciplines for five more years, at the end of which Prajāpati, now finding Indra to have made himself fully competent, gave him the highest knowledge. At long last, Indra not only understood the Ātman intellectually but experienced his own identity as the Ātman, the true self beyond the body, the mind, the senses, and the ego. All of Indra's doubts were dispelled and the knots of ignorance binding his heart were cut asunder for ever.

This story from the Chāndogya Upaniṣad (8.7.1–8.12.6) illustrates some important points. First, it emphasizes the need for competence (*adhikāra*) to know and realize spiritual truths. It is significant that Prajāpati did not even ask Indra and Virocana the purpose of their visit until they had spent thirty-two years under discipline. Why "thirty-two"? I don't know. The number doesn't matter, except to convey the idea that without sufficient preparation we cannot really benefit from a teaching. A seed planted in a barren and infertile soil cannot fructify unless the soil is prepared well with water and adequate nutrients.

Secondly, the story makes an obvious point: there are differences in the aptitudes and capacities of those seeking knowledge. No two people are alike. Indra and Virocana were quite different from one another. What made sense to Virocana made no sense to Indra. Another important point the story stresses is that the knowledge gained is directly proportional to the fitness of the student. Virocana could get only what he could understand and assimilate according to his capacity (which was small) and his stage of development (which was rudimentary), hence his knowledge remained superficial. Indra's case was different. After repeated disciplines and deep reflection (which increased his capacity and deepened his understanding), Indra became fit to receive the highest knowledge and Prajāpati gave it to Indra after assessing his competence.

Yet another factor is the value of asking questions.[1] Indra's questions revealed the direction of his thinking and the roadblocks in his reasoning. The quality of the questions we ask depends on the clarity of our minds. As our understanding deepens, our questions become clearer and more refined. Good teachers seldom spoon-feed their students. They don't give answers but provide enough hints so that the students can make their own discoveries and achieve their own breakthroughs. Lastly, the story also shows that it is possible to lead a student to the highest truth in a phased manner, provided the student aspires to go higher and is prepared to work for it, as Indra was.

All these ideas find expression in one of the fundamental tenets of Hinduism called *adhikāri-vāda*, the principle of competence. The recognition of differences in individuals, in their fitness and aspirations, has historically made Hindus tolerant, patient and accepting. Swami Vivekananda referred to these outstanding characteristics in his inaugural address in 1893 at the World's Parliament of Religions in Chicago. He said, "I am proud to belong to a religion which has taught the world both tolerance and universal acceptance. We believe not only in universal toleration, but we accept all religions as true" (CW 1. 3).

Acknowledging the need of different minds to approach Truth in a manner specifically suited to each, a Vedic sage could boldly proclaim: "Truth is one, the wise describe it variously" (Ṛg-Veda, 1.164.46). The Truth is one but the paths leading to that Truth can be many. That is what Sri Ramakrishna meant when he said, "There are as many paths (to the Truth) as there are faiths." Not only are the paths diverse, but those walking on the paths are also diverse. That is how the principle of competence gave rise to the concept of the chosen deity (*iṣṭa-devatā*), leaving the spiritual seekers free to worship the form and aspect of Truth that appealed to them, and also gave them the freedom to choose the way or method that suited their temperaments and capacities.

Such broadness of vision gave Hindus considerable power and freedom to embrace diverse ways of thinking and doing. Innumerable tribes and conquerors crossed the Indian frontier to loot and to rule. They brought with them their own cultural characteristics, religious beliefs and customs, superstitions and traditions. Besides the social, political and economic upheavals created by those incursions, they introduced even more diversity in the Hindu world. The attackers and the colonizers who stayed long enough were assimilated into the social and cultural fabric of the subcontinent, their personalities now a happy amalgam of Hindu characteristics and their own inherent qualities. Those that went away after a short stay carried with them some of the ideas they learnt in the process and enriched their own native cultures.

This is how religious consciousness or "the eternal way of life" (*sanātana dharma*) evolves, rejecting none and accepting all in its wide embrace, with a word of cheer and encouragement to every soul struggling in the gymnasium of the world. Freedom is the necessary condition of growth.[2] The inheritors of the Vedic traditions grew and developed spiritually because of the freedom they enjoyed on the spiritual plane. Vedānta, the science and philosophy that undergirds the Vedic wisdom, has freedom as its principle. In fact, it identifies the ultimate goal itself with absolute freedom (*mukti* or *mokṣa*).

The principle of competence was applied even in the selection of students, as is evident from Indra and Virocana's story. It is necessary—imperative really—that the aptitude and capacity of students be rightly assessed before the training begins, so the teacher can guide them individually along the path and in a way that fits their needs. Only a structured training regimen, suited to the specific strengths of every student, can ensure success.

There are innumerable instances in the Upaniṣads, the Purāṇas and other ancient books where the teachers tested their students before teaching them.

We read in the Kaṭhopaniṣad (1.1.23-29) that Yama tests Naciketā to ascertain his fitness for the knowledge of Brahman. Yama offers Naciketā horses, elephants and cattle, children and grandchildren, rulership of the earth and a long life, heavenly dancers and numerous other desirable things which are beyond the reach of mere mortals. But Naciketā is an *adhikārī* of the highest order and, realizing the transitory nature of those apparently covetable treasures, he spurns them all and seeks only the knowledge of Brahman. Yama is overjoyed to see such a supremely competent student and teaches him the highest Truth. Since Naciketā is a fit *adhikārī* and receives instructions from Yama, who is a competent teacher, Naciketā becomes free from ignorance and death, and attains Brahman (2.3.18).

In other Upaniṣads too we find severe tests and disciplines to which the teachers subjected their students: Pratardana was tested by Indra (Kauśitaki Upaniṣad, 3.1), Janaśruti Pautrāyaṇa by Raikva (Chāndogya Upaniṣad, 4.1), Aruṇi by Pravāhana (Bṛhadāraṇyaka Upaniṣad, 6.2.6), Janaka by Yājñavalkya (Bṛhadāraṇyaka Upaniṣad, 4.3.1), and Bṛhadratha by Śākayanya (Maitrāyaṇi Upaniṣad, 1.2). In the Praśna Upanishad (9.2) we come across the sage Pippalāda who told his six disciples to practice austerities and celibacy for one full year before he asked them any questions.

The tradition of teachers testing the competency of students is ancient, and it persists to this day not only across religious traditions but also in secular education. Sri Ramakrishna tested those that wanted to be his disciples and asked that they test him as well. Only after he was satisfied by his examination would he accept them and train them on their path. That is why we find that he had established a distinct relationship with every one of them, and the methods he employed and the instructions he gave varied according to the need and capability of each disciple. For instance, he encouraged young Narendra to read the nondualistic text *Aṣṭāvakra Saṁhitā*, while he warned the other disciples not to even peep into that book at that stage of their spiritual life.

Most classical Vedānta texts usually describe the basic qualities essential to make a student fit for the study. Many of the Upaniṣads, and books like the Brahma Sūtras, the Gītā, *Vivekacūdāmaṇi*, *Upadeśa-sāhasri*, and *Vedānta-sāra,* lay down a number of preliminary conditions that the student is expected to fulfill if the study of those books is to be fruitful. It is imperative to be a fit student before beginning the study. The conditions laid down and the disciplines enjoined are more or less similar in every case, requiring the student to be selfless, develop spiritual aspiration, and practice physical and mental disciplines.

The Shift from Competence to Eligibility

Everything tends to degenerate with time—things get old and break down, we too get old and eventually die, ideas become diluted or outdated, and principles get compromised or are abandoned. Alongside the brightness of positive tendencies in human nature resides the darkness of negative tendencies. The two opposites manage to coexist in an awkward balance. Our world is filled with such pairs of opposites—birth and death, good and bad, knowledge and ignorance, love and hate —and there is no way to avoid them unless we somehow transcend our present existence. Reformers come in every generation to prevent the darkness from taking over everything totally. Not that it can but, unless prevented, it can make the world a hellish experience, especially for those who are spiritually sensitive.

It is not surprising therefore that, down the centuries, the principle of competence became diluted when it fell into the hands of those who were themselves not competent. Compromises were made and the principle was misused and abused.

Spiritual life has two basic components: study and practice. In other words, it involves *knowing* what spiritual life is and then *practicing* it daily. Experience is the ultimate source of knowledge but, to get knowledge, we initially turn to two sources—texts and teachers. Knowledge is power, so those who have knowledge become powerful. The desire to retain power and to exert it to one's advantage was the prime reason that the principle of competence became abused.

How did they do it? By controlling access to knowledge. This was accomplished by placing restrictions on textual study (not everyone was deemed eligible to study) and access to teachers (not everyone was deemed eligible to be taught). To be sure, not everyone placed such restrictions, but many did. The principle of competence gradually became transformed into the condition for eligibility —a subtle shift, but one with devastating consequences.

Why would anyone want to do this? In addition to the desire to reap personal benefit, fear certainly played a part. If knowledge became easily available, the custodians of knowledge couldn't hold on to their power and position and the privileges that resulted from them. History is replete with examples of people who could not resist clinging to power, position and privilege. Because of this, effort was made to keep the highest knowledge hidden from others. The excuse was that most people were incompetent, they wouldn't be able to grasp the teachings, and their distorted understanding would create no end of trouble to themselves and to society.

Thus the powers that be restricted the flow of knowledge to a select few, which predictably included their own families and those in their inner circle. For others, they introduced a plethora of local customs and observances so as to provide something easily practicable and digestible. As a result, mostly meaningless rituals and superstitions proliferated, and people held on to these tenaciously with the firm belief that those were the core of spiritual life.

This state of affairs did not go unchallenged. There were reformers in every generation who militated against the restrictions and tried to lift them or to go around them. They had mixed success, but the fight continued between the so-called orthodox imposing restrictions and the liberals trying to remove them. Swami Vivekananda was among those who tried to throw open the door of the highest knowledge to one and all. He strongly resented the idea that spiritual teachings should remain a property monopolized over by a privileged few. He said:

> It shall no more be a *rahasya,* a secret; it shall no more live with monks in caves and forests, and in the Himalayas; it must come down to the daily, everyday life of the people; it shall be worked out in the palace of the king, in the cave of the recluse; it shall be worked out in the cottage of the poor, by the beggar in the street, everywhere; anywhere it can be worked out. Therefore do not fear whether you are a woman or a Sudra, for this religion is so great, says Lord Krishna, that even a little of it brings a great amount of good. (CW 3. 427)

Wherever and whenever Vivekananda found human beings suppressed, exploited and trampled upon, he was among the first who protested. He saw that the sublime and rational principle of competence had fallen into incompetent hands and they had made a travesty of it by withholding the light of knowledge and, in its stead, introducing superstitions and customs which were "a mass of meaningless nonsense" (CW 5. 263).

While the earlier thinkers had stressed the objective differences between people, Swami Vivekananda emphasized their subjective unity as the Ātman, the innermost true self, pure and free by nature, and the repository of all knowledge. Given the right training and opportunities, it is possible for every person to manifest their intrinsic purity and knowledge. No one can be considered lost at any stage of evolution. If some are considered weak or unfit for higher knowledge, they deserve more attention and care, not less, than what is given to those who are strong and competent.

Vivekananda accepted the principle of competence, but pointed out that it did not justify the neglect of, and indifference to, the vast majority of people labeled as unfit for higher knowledge. He thus infused great hope into the heart of all by emphasizing the divinity of the human soul.

Another important point Swami Vivekananda stressed was that light could never bring greater darkness, knowledge could never lead us to greater ignorance:

> Knowledge means freedom from the errors which ignorance leads to. Knowledge paving the way to error! Enlightenment leading to confusion! Is it possible? We are not bold enough to speak out broad truths for fear of losing the respect of the people... Preach the highest

> truths broadcast. Do not fear losing your respect or causing unhappy friction. (CW 5. 264)

By pointing out the divinity of the soul and the infinite possibilities that lay hidden in it, and by showing the enlightening nature of knowledge, Vivekananda freed the principle of competence from the unhealthy accretions it had gathered during the course of the last few centuries.

When Swami Vivekananda referred to this principle as "the outcome of pure selfishness" (CW, 5. 263), he was referring to its distorted version that was in vogue and had reached its peak in the nineteenth century. He showed in his own life how the principle of competence could be adopted in its pure and unalloyed form in training the disciples. Sister Christine, one of his Western disciples, later wrote of him:

> His method was different with each disciple. With some, it was an incessant hammering. The severest asceticism was imposed with regard to diet, habits, even clothing and conversation. With others ... the habit of asceticism was not encouraged... With one the method was ridicule—loving ridicule—with another it was sternness... By all these means the process of evolution was accelerated, and the whole nature was transmuted.[3]

Swami Vivekananda had to address innumerable groups of people everywhere. He was aware that his audiences comprised men and women of varying capacities and temperaments. But he had a mission to fulfill. He knew intuitively that the teachings he was giving were not meant only for the groups that sat before him, but would also help the succeeding generations of spiritual seekers. He therefore gave expression to the highest truths before one and all.

He did not expect all to appreciate and assimilate at once his bold message. Nor was it necessary. During one of his class talks in America, someone from the audience said to him. "Swami, I don't agree with you." He turned to her and said, "Madam, it was not meant for you." Another said, "But, Swami, I feel the truth of it." "Ah! Then it was for you!" he exclaimed. Vivekananda knew that, when people evolved spiritually, they would be able to see more light and meaning into his words.

A Template for Spiritual Fitness

The principle of competence plays a major role in the way spiritual training is given and received. We have seen how the principle matured during the Vedic period and, in more recent centuries, was misused by some to impose arbitrary conditions of eligibility to determine who can be taught and given access to resources. Many of those conditions have become irrelevant today with the easy availability of books and the advent of the internet. Today the access to texts and teachers is no longer restricted the way it once was. It is virtually impossible now to meaningfully deny access to resources. All of this has added another layer of personal responsibility for every potential student.

But lack or denial of access is never really the only hurdle. Merely having access to all the resources in the world doesn't in itself guarantee success. The simple truth is that we can take in only as much as we can digest —and only what we truly digest can nourish us and make us stronger. At its heart, the principle of competence simply means that the benefit we derive is directly related to the capacity we have. Luckily, our capacity to take in and to digest is not a fixed quantity. We have the ability to develop and deepen our capacity. Our ability to benefit from the available resources can increase if we work hard, it can also decrease if we are negligent. The practice demands constant attention and care.

Terms such as fitness, competency and capacity convey an idea, but it's still somewhat vague. If we need to work on our spiritual fitness, we need something more concrete. Vedānta texts provide a template for every seeker of truth to measure their spiritual fitness. It is traditionally known as Four Practices (*sādhana-catuṣṭaya*). Because these are basic to Vedānta study and practice, they will be referred to throughout this book as Four Basic Practices. Traditionally, they are stated in the following order:

1. Discernment (*viveka*)
2. Non-attachment (*vairāgya*)
3. "Six Treasures" (*ṣaṭ-sampatti*)
4. Longing for Freedom (*mumukṣutva*)

Spiritual fitness can be assessed on the basis of these four practices. How well I do these practices determines how much of nourishment I can truly absorb from the spiritual resources available to me.

The goal of spiritual life is freedom (*mokṣa*). I can attain the goal only if and when I am fit to attain it. Acquiring fitness, or becoming an *adhikārī*, should therefore be my primary concern. Sometimes the goal can appear so fascinating, its description so intellectually captivating and emotionally fulfilling, that I may delude myself into thinking that I'm already there, instead of investing enough time and energy in doing what needs to be done to reach the goal. Swami Vivekananda referred to this tendency as "our great defect in life":

> Our great defect in life is that we are so much drawn to the ideal, the goal is so much more enchanting, so much more alluring, so much bigger in our mental horizon, that we lose sight of the details altogether. But whenever failure comes, if we analyze it critically, in ninety-nine per cent of cases we shall find that it was because we did not pay attention to the means. Proper attention to the finishing, strengthening, of the means is what we need. With the means all right, the end must come. (CW 2. 1)

The means is to become a fit student—and to measure how close I am to being fit (or how far from it), I have the Four Basic Practices. My spiritual journey really begins when I make persistent effort to cast my life in the mould of an ideal student. The very first thing needed is a sincere and correct self-appraisal. I should know where I stand. How can I start on a journey without knowing where I am, where I want to go, and which the best way is to reach my destination?

Self-appraisal is not easy. We think we know who we are. Nothing could be more deceptive. Most people know more about others than about themselves. An objective assessment is relatively easy. What makes self-examination difficult is the need to objectify one's own self. It's almost like getting out of myself to take a hard look at who I am. But self-examination will produce only erroneous results if the ego is too strong. Some amount of ego-reduction is necessary for an accurate self-assessment. A distorted self-perception is like looking at one's image in a convex or a concave mirror (or worse, in a mirror which is a twisted combination of both). People have either an exaggerated and bloated image of their virtues and capacities, or a highly diminished view of their capabilities and strengths. Both are dangerous. The former usually takes the form of vanity and arrogance; the latter, of self-depreciation and false humility.

It is helpful to remember that humility does not consist in repeatedly telling myself and others, "I am a nobody. I know nothing." If I persist with this practice, it may turn out to be a self-fulfilling prophecy, and I am likely to remain all my life a "nobody" who knows "nothing." True humility comes from a position of strength, not weakness. It consists in a genuine spirit of surrender to God and only a spiritually strong person can be truly humble.

We have therefore to steer ourselves clear from these dangers that lie in self-examination. We don't have to share our findings with others, but we can at least be honest with ourselves. Every one of us has both strengths as well as weaknesses. It is tempting to showcase our strengths and hide our weaknesses. That's a futile exercise though, since our strengths and weaknesses are revealed to others anyway through the way we live and especially in our unguarded moments.

What others think of me is not as important as what I think of myself. Do I really know who I am? If I can have some idea at least of my strengths and weaknesses, I shall have a personal frame of reference to help me understand what I ought to do to become a better student than who I am at present.

I can be whoever I want to be, and I can reach whatever goal I set for myself, provided I first acquire spiritual fitness. To that end, I need to take a close look at each of the Four Basic Practices to examine how I can practice them in my own life. It is to discernment, the first of these practices, that we now turn in the following chapter.

CHAPTER 3

discernment

The practice of discernment (*viveka*) is the simple practice of looking in order to figure out what's what. We do it all the time, which is how we are able to make decisions in life. When we are able to distinguish right from wrong, or good from bad, most of us choose to do what is right or what is good. Another criterion we use is to do what is in our best interest, or what makes us happy and helps us avoid pain and suffering. It is obvious that we need to look and think in order to determine what makes sense and what doesn't, what is right and what isn't, what is worth pursuing and what isn't.

As the first of the Four Basic Practices though, discernment is not merely the practice of looking and deciding, but looking *deeply and carefully* and only then deciding. This makes a huge difference. Sometimes we don't look long enough or deep enough and sometimes we are in too great a hurry. The decisions made without sufficient thought often misfire and we end up doing things that we later regret. We have all made such mistakes sometime or other, perhaps often.

It is true that we may not always have the luxury of time. Sometimes we are required to take split-second decisions. There *is* no time to think then. We just have to go with our gut. But such situations are rare. Most decisions in life don't have to be made instantly. If we take our time, if we pause to take a deep breath and look carefully, we may notice things that we may have missed. *Looking deeply and carefully is at the heart of discernment.* Only when we look deeply do we see the nuances and the subtleties involved. That increases our chances of choosing well. When our choices are wise, we suffer less and rejoice more.

But there is more to discernment than simply avoiding pain and being happy. When looking deeply becomes a habit, we notice that things are not always how they appear to be. What feels like a good thing may, upon close observation, turn out to be not so good. What feels worthless at first sight may be found to be valuable when we take a closer look. This teaches us to not be taken in by appearances. When we begin to see things as they truly are, we are able to make good decisions.

Something more happens as well: because we now notice things that we had missed before, we inevitably start asking the kind of questions we did not ask before. Discernment is like deep sea diving: under water we encounter a new world, a world that was not visible on the surface. Looking deeply also reveals to us a new world. We see others with a new pair of eyes. The world *feels* different.

Naturally, questions will arise. I may look at a chair and begin to wonder—is this object anything more than material particles somehow held together in a form which is assigned a name in every language? I may look at the world and ask—is the world simply an expansive ocean of atoms and molecules, or protons and electrons, held in place by various forces? What makes the people around me different from "objects"? Why are people and animals classified as "living" and the chair before me is "nonliving"? When I meet a friend, I am really seeing a physical body which is responsive and looks conscious. Is my friend simply a body? What about the friend's mind and the intellect? Are those material too? Is there anything at all which is *not* material?

The practice of looking deeply may fuel in my heart the urge to know if life has any ultimate purpose beyond my efforts to make the most of life until I am devoured by death. I may want to know who this "me" is for whose sake I do whatever I do. Unless I figure out who this "me" is, how can I make sense of whatever is seen as "mine"? Does the "me" survive death? If it does, then who really dies? Also, where does this "me" disappear to when I'm asleep? What is this mysterious movie called "dreams" that I see every night? How does a dream manage to appear as real to me as the world I'm seeing at present? The world I see when I am awake vanishes when I sleep, and my dream world vanishes when I wake up. Neither the waking world nor the dream world persists without break, so why do I think of one as real and the other as unreal? Are these two worlds *really* different?

Most of these questions, and their possible answers, can be unsettling. They can shatter my present understanding of both my own self as well as the world around me. Looking deeply is beneficial, but looking *too* deeply may not be everyone's cup of tea. Deep sea diving is not for everyone. I may want to return to the surface and waddle in the muddy waters of this world again in order to resume my shallow life—and most of us do just that. Discernment is an exciting practice, but it is difficult to persevere in it without patience, courage, and most importantly, faith in oneself. The practice of discernment is for heroes, not for cowards. It is for the brave, not for the faint of heart.

If I have confidence in myself, I won't be afraid to explore uncharted waters. When I begin to look deeply at myself, it becomes obvious that over the years my body has been growing and changing continually. The same with my mind—my ideas, hopes, feelings, fears, memories have been changing, evolving. In the midst of all these changes, I still feel I am the same person. Something has remained unchanged within me. The unchanged part is the "real me." Separating it from everything that is changing, separating the real from the transient, is a gift of discernment.

Way back when, a revolutionary discovery was made and it was this—*the unchanging is infinite.* It is birthless and deathless, pure and perfect, utterly free and unfettered. It is nonmaterial, hence laws of matter don't apply to it. Being infinite, it is one and undivided. In stark contrast, everything around me is diverse and divided. It begins at some point and it ends sooner or later. Everything in the world depends on everything else. Things are interconnected by the inexorable law of cause and effect. My real self, Ātman, is conscious, infinite and eternal, whereas the world is material, temporary and transient. The Ātman is real. Compared to it, everything else feels illusory. It is this distinction between the real and the illusory, the unchanging and the constantly changing, that we have the power to see if we continue to look deeply with patience and perseverance, courage and determination.

The implications of this discovery are staggeringly magical. When we experience reality unfiltered by the mind and the senses, everything that limits us in life disappears. Fear of death vanishes. We forget what stress and anxiety feel like. We are immersed in bliss, filled with love, and experience unimaginable freedom. This is not a pie-in-the-sky fable. This is what others before us have directly experienced. A record of what they discovered is found in the Upaniṣads, which are the primary source of Vedānta. This is not a matter of *believing* what some texts say. Whatever they say is open to testing. We can verify the truth for ourselves. Throw blind acceptance out the window! Swami Vivekananda's powerful words come to mind:

> [True religion] is not talk, or doctrines, or theories; nor is it sectarianism . . . Religion does not consist in erecting temples, or building churches, or attending public worship. It is not to be found in books, or in words, or in lectures, or in organizations. Religion consists in realization. (CW 4. 179-80)

If the Ātman is real, we must experience it for ourselves. Simply reading about it in books is not enough. We don't have to accept God merely on faith. If God exists, we must see him! Nothing less will do. Nothing else can satisfy us fully.

> [We] must realize God, feel God, see God, talk to God. That is religion. (CW 4. 165).

The practice of religion begins with discernment. That is the first step, and the most important one. Every journey begins with the first step. If I want to practice discernment, how do I go about it? There are a few common-sense things I can try to do:

1. *Quieting.* A regular practice of prayer, repetition of mantra (*japa*), and meditation often leads to a state of inner quiet. This can last for a while but usually fades away when we get busy with our daily chores. With sustained practice, it is possible to summon the inner quiet at will—and this greatly helps in the practice of looking deeply.

2. *Withdrawing.* We all have our biases and prejudices, our own special likes and dislikes. These can get in the way of decision-making and vitiate the process. It is helpful to remain as neutral as possible when we look deeply at anything to understand it well.
3. *Deciding.* After a careful study, it is easier to make an assessment with confidence. The conclusion we reach helps us decide what should (or should not) be done next.

The blessing of always looking deeply at everything far outweighs the challenges that arise in the practice—and challenges there will be plenty if we take the practice to heart. As we have seen, the practice of discernment raises questions that may not have immediate answers, but it is the rigorous search for the answers that makes life meaningful and worth living. It brings depth and stability that is missing in the superficiality of our present life. As the reality begins to unfold and our blinkers disappear, a new world is revealed. The old me fades away. A new me, the real me, takes its place. The practice of Vedānta begins with discernment, or looking deeply, and it ends with me discovering myself, my *true* self.

Because the practice of discernment ultimately leads to seeing the distinction between the real and the unreal, or between the eternal and the transient, Vedānta texts define discernment in those terms. See, for instance, Śrī Śaṅkarācārya's *Aparokṣānubhūti* ("Direct Experience"), verse 5:

नित्यमात्मस्वरूपं हि दृश्यं तद्विपरीतगम् ।

एवं यो निश्चयः सम्यग्विवेको वस्तुनः स वै ॥

Nityaṁ ātma-svarūpaṁ hi dṛśyaṁ tad viparīta-gam, / Evaṁ yo niścayaḥ samyag-viveko vastunaḥ sa vai.

Discernment is the firm determination that the Ātman alone is eternal and whatever is seen is indeed its opposite (in other words, transient).

Sometimes discernment becomes defined not in terms of the Ātman but in terms of Brahman, the reality underlying everything. When we think of what is real in an individual, we call it Ātman. When we think of what is real in the entire universe, we call it Brahman. What is real inside is not different from what is real outside. Reality is one. The two, Brahman and Ātman, are identical.

In Sadānanda Yogīndra's 15th century text *Vedānta-sāra* ("The Essence of Vedānta"), discernment between the eternal and the transient is defined thus:

ब्रह्मैव नित्यं वस्तु, ततोऽन्यदखिलमनित्यमिति ।

Brahma-eva nityaṁ vastu, tato anyad-akhilam-anityam-iti.

Brahman alone is eternally real, everything else is transient.

Sri Ramakrishna expressed the same truth in different words—and this teaching of his occurs frequently in his conversations with disciples. "God alone is real," he repeatedly told them, and often added, “all else is illusory” or “the world is unsubstantial, like a dream” (*Gospel of Sri Ramakrishna,* 396, 400, 421, 788, 911).

It is the conscious practice of discernment that launches us on an exciting journey. Even before we can fully discern that God alone is real and everything else is illusory, we discover a lot of things when we look deeply into our experiences. For instance, we will notice that buried under our daily experience of joy and sorrow is a deeper experience of extremely subtle suffering. It is existential, in the sense that it is inseparable from our very *existence* as human beings. It was this suffering that made Krishna refer to the world as “joyless” (Gītā 9. 33) and “an abode of suffering” (Gītā 8. 15). This is also why the first among the Four Noble Truths taught by Buddha is, “Life is suffering.”

This suffering is not limited only to *this* world. It is present wherever we may be, in heaven or hell, or in any of the celestial worlds, since the suffering is caused by our limitations in a body and mind, and the inevitable inequalities and injustices involved in collective living. Discernment helps us reject even heaven as a worthwhile goal since it cannot provide total freedom from suffering.

The only way to overcome suffering is to experience the infinite reality of God, or the true self, which eliminates our transient and false human identity and reveals our eternal and true identity. We then experience eternal bliss. It is also existential, in the sense that it is inseparable from our our very *existence* as divine beings.

The practice of discernment begins in a simple way, separating the good from the bad and the right from the wrong. When we continue to look deeply and carefully at everything, within ourselves and also around us, we see a new "me" and a new world. If we are able to keep doing that and not turn away, it leads to the experience God, the eternal being, the reality behind all appearances, and discovering it to be not different from the true inner self.

Such is the primacy of discernment that Śrī Śaṅkarācārya called it "the crest jewel" (*cūḍāmaṇi*) of Vedānta practice in his celebrated text *Vivekacūḍāmaṇi*. Perhaps it was not an accident of history that the greatest Vedānta teacher of our own time came to be known as Vivekananda, "the bliss of discernment."

CHAPTER 4

non-attachment

We have seen that discernment is the practice of looking deeply in order to see things as they truly are. This helps us distinguish right from wrong, good from bad, healthy from unhealthy. The analysis helps in decision-making—and the decision generally is to choose what is right, what is good or what is healthy. We instinctively attach ourselves to whatever makes us happy and detach from whatever makes us unhappy. Thus detachment is a natural follow-up to discernment, and is the second among the Four Basic Practices.

The Sanskrit word, *vairāgya,* is often understood as "detachment," but this word has a different flavor in English than what *vairāgya* has in Sanskrit. The nouns *vairāgya* and *virāga* refer to the state from which "attachment is gone," derived as they are from *rāga* ("attachment") and the prefix *vi* (in the sense of *vigata,* "has gone"). Swami Vivekananda mostly used the word "non-attachment," which comes closer to the literal meaning of *vairāgya*. While "non-attachment" clearly means the absence of attachment, "detachment" may also imply indifference to others, which is not what *vairāgya* is about. Whichever way we choose to translate *vairāgya*, it is helpful to keep in mind that the practice is primarily about inner change, not outer actions.

The roots of attachment lie deep in the awareness of "I" and "mine." My *primary* attachment is to everything I identify as "I" (usually my body and often mind as well). My *secondary* attachment is to everything I identify as "mine" (my family, friends, possessions, ideas, feelings, and so much more). Whatever I am identified with becomes a kind of extension of myself—it becomes either "me" or "mine." Whatever happens to me or to mine affects me, since I react as if it were happening to my own self or to those I see as my own. I react positively if it makes me happy, and negatively if it makes me unhappy.

Bobbing up and down with life's currents becomes the norm. The story of our lives is the story of doing a lot, undoing some of it later, and re-doing everything else most of the time. While we're at it, we keep shuttling between happiness and sorrow. Speaking in New York on December 18, 1895, Swami Vivekananda pointed out how nature toys with us as a cat sometimes does with a mouse:

> This moment we are whipped, and when we begin to weep, nature gives us a dollar; again we are whipped,

> and when we weep, nature gives us a piece of ginger-bread, and we begin to laugh again. (CW, I. 411)

Isn't there more to life than endlessly going back and forth between happiness and sorrow? That is what attachment does to us.

It is important to have a clear understanding of what attachment is, because attachment is often mistaken for love. Superficially, love and attachment do seem connected if not identical. If I love someone, wouldn't I be attached to that person?—one might say. Through discernment we learn that not only are love and attachment different, they are in fact incompatible. They are mutually opposed to each other in two significant ways. First, the person in the grip of attachment is primarily attached to "I", whereas one who is truly in love seldom thinks of the "I"—it's all about "you," the object one's love. Secondly, the person who is attached to "I" wants to own people and things and make them "mine," whereas the one in love respects freedom, so no one is tied with the noose of ownership.

The difference between attachment and love becomes even more clear when we look at the results they produce. Attachment can, and often does, lead to dependence, anxiety, anger, jealousy, and stress. In stark contrast, true love leads to deeper happiness and greater freedom. Most relationships produce both happiness and anxiety, a curious mixture of freedom and bondage, fulfillment and deprivation—which means most relationships are a mixture of love and attachment, each producing its results. Through discernment and experience we realize sooner or later that the more detached we are from our instinctive clinging to "I," the more we are able to love. Non-attachment and love go together, no matter how odd that may sound to our conventional way of thinking.

The best we can hope for through our various attachments are passing sensations of happiness interrupted by sorrow. This kind of punctuated happiness brings no lasting fulfillment. Most of us realize this, but have no clue what to do about it. If we care to practice discernment, we soon find out that the world is transient and joyless (Gītā, 9. 33) and really an abode of sorrow (Gītā, 8. 15). If we can see this "defect" in the world (Gītā, 13. 8), detaching from it should be easy, especially when we learn that life beyond the duality of joy and sorrow is a life of total freedom, perfection and bliss. But our patterns of thinking and doing are difficult to overcome, since they are continually reinforced by mental impressions generated by our own thoughts and actions. It's a vicious loop.

Considering how tough it is to subdue the desire for enjoyment of the earthly pleasures around us, we can only imagine how nearly impossible it would be to reject the pleasures of heaven, which are believed to be thousands of time more alluring than what the mind can even imagine at present. But that is the level of detachment required in order to be spiritually illumined. As Śaṅkarācārya's *Aparokṣānubhūti* ("Direct Experience") says, the objects of enjoyment even in the highest of heavens should appear as "the excreta of a crow" to the spiritual seeker. The *Vivekacūḍāmaṇi*, 21, defines detachment as aversion to any sense contact with "the ephemeral objects of enjoyment ranging from one's own body to the celestial world of Brahmā."

"The less you are attached to the world, the more you love God," as Sri Ramakrishna pointed out (*Gospel*, 277). If we can find ways to consciously increase our love for God —to become "attached" to the spiritual ideal, so to speak —the easier it gets to detach from everything else. There are also other things we can try to do. Since "I" is at the root of all our problems—including our stresses, worries and anxieties—the practice primarily involves finding ways to detach from the ego. When the ego is absent, as in deep sleep, we have no problems. Come morning, we wake up, the ego returns, and the problems return too. Is it possible to be awake, to have the sense of "I" and yet be free from all attachments and the accompanying problems?

There are at least two ways to practice non-attachment, which serve the two ways most people tend to think of God, or the Supreme Being, or the transcendent reality, or whichever other way we may think of the spiritual ideal. We can think of the Divine either in a personal way (meaning, someone with qualities and form, or simply with qualities) or in an impersonal way (that is, without any form or qualities).

Those with an impersonal view have to rely on their own steadfastness and will-power to do what is right in every situation. For them, every moment and every action can be converted into an occasion to be reminded of the ideal (CW, I. III). They have to strive to remember that doing what is right and what is good is the only way to spiritual freedom. They do what is right simply because it is the right thing to do (Gītā, 18. 9). They do what is good because it is good to do good, and for no other reason. There must be no other motive, no expectation, no self-interest involved in their actions. This is tough but doable if there is both intense desire and an unswerving determination to hold on to everything that is good and true. The goal is to do this *all* the time and in *every* situation, not merely when it is convenient to do so.

Those with a personal view of God strive to be mindful of doing everything out of love for God (Gītā, 9. 27). Even if they have worked hard to acquire their knowledge, skills and talents, they recognize that all of those are really gifts from God. Without God's grace, they wouldn't have had the energy and wisdom to accomplish anything. Since they acknowledge that their very existence depends on God, they offer to God all their activities as well as the results. They choose to be instruments, not agents, of action. Non-attachment occurs naturally in their lives, since they see that nothing really belongs to them. God does everything, not them. Everything happens through God's will, not theirs. The more they surrender to the divine will, the more non-attached they naturally become.

These, then, are two powerful and effective ways of practicing non-attachment: (1) doing work for work's sake, and

(2) doing work as an offering to God. Both these methods effectively eliminate the mischief played by the ego. They bring not only peace and joy but also transcendence, which leads to true freedom, perfection and total fearlessness.

Everything in the world is fraught with fear. Only non-attachment makes us fearless. This is described grippingly in Bhartṛhari's 5th century text, *Vairāgya Śatakam* ("A Hundred Verses on Non-attachment"), 31:

भोगे रोगभयं कुले च्युतिभयं वित्ते नृपालाद्भयं

माने दैन्यभयं बले रिपुभयं रूपे जराया भयम् ।

शास्त्रे वादिभयं गुणे खलभयं काये कृतान्ताद्भयं

सर्वं वस्तु भयान्वितं भुवि नृणां वैराग्यमेवाभयम् ॥

Bhoge roga-bhayaṁ kule cyuti-bhayaṁ vitte nṛpālād bhayaṁ / māne dainya-bhayaṁ bale ripu-bhayaṁ rūpe jarāyā bhayam; / Śāstre vādi-bhayaṁ guṇe khala-bhayaṁ kāye kṛtāntād-bhayaṁ / sarvaṁ vastu bhayānvitaṁ bhuvi nṛṇāṁ vairāgyam-eva abhayam.

In sensual enjoyment, there is the fear of disease; in social status, the fear of a downfall; in wealth, the fear of (hostile) kings; in honor, the fear of humiliation; in power, the fear of enemies; in beauty, the fear of aging, in scholarship, the fear of opponents; in virtue, the fear of slanderers; in body, the fear of death. Everything in this world of humans is smeared with fear. Detachment alone brings fearlessness.

Discernment and non-attachment are connected. Each fulfills the other. Together, they are powerful. Separated, they are meaningless. Discernment without non-attachment is pointless, and non-attachment without discernment is rudderless. Spiritual life truly begins only when discernment and non-attachment join hands. They make it possible to attain the "six treasures," the next in our study of the Four Basic Practices.

CHAPTER 5

"six treasures"

The "six treasures" (*ṣaṭ-sampatti*) is not really one practice but six distinct practices, namely, restraining the mind, restraining the senses, pulling the mind and the senses back, forbearance, concentration, and deep faith. So why have these practices been clubbed together and treated as if the collection is a single practice?

The reason is that each of these "treasures" is closely connected with the others. They all provide mutual support to one another and each enhances the practice of others. While this is true for all of the Four Basic Practices, it is especially so in the case of the practices included in the "six treasures."

The Kaṭha Upaniṣad (1.3.3–8) offers the imagery of a chariot. We are told that the body is the chariot and the Ātman is the master seated in the chariot. The intellect is the charioteer, the mind is the rein, the senses are the horses, and the sense objects are the road. For the master of the chariot to reach the destination, it is important that the charioteer be alert and holds the rein tightly, for this keeps the horses under control and on the road to the destination. If the charioteer is distracted and the reins are slack, the horses will bolt and the chariot will likely go off the road and crash.

Every aspect in the imagery—the chariot, the charioteer, the reins, and the horses—is important for the safety of the master riding in the chariot. They all depend on each other for the success of the journey. The chariot ride is seemingly one activity, but really comprises a bunch of things—the charioteer practicing alertness, holding the reins with confidence, and controlling the horses so that they stay on the road and take the chariot to the destination. All of these things need to go right in order for the ride to be comfortable. In the same way, all six practices that comprise the "six treasures" depend on each other for doing what they do.

Let's begin with restraining the mind and see how it is essential for others in the "six treasures" pack. Trying to restrain the senses with an unrestrained mind is a futile exercise. When the mind is spread thin, identifying with the family, friends, possessions, and other interests, it can neither have total commitment to the ideal nor have faith in the practices to reach that ideal. Given the propensity of latent tendencies, it is difficult to practice pulling back the mind when it is distracted unless the mind is habituated to being controlled. How can an unrestrained mind be made to practice concentration? Only a disciplined mind can bear the ups and downs of life without complaining, hence restraint is needed even for the practice of forbearance.

We'll see that the practice of restraining the senses also supports the other practices. Restraining the mind becomes so much easier when the senses are restrained, and vice versa. The two forms of restraint reinforce and support each other. Deep faith, concentration, and withdrawing the mind are impossible for a person whose senses are not controlled. Forbearance is greatly supported by a diligent restraint of the senses.

Sometimes the restraint of the mind and the senses fails due to a powerful mental impression which has resurrected a past habit. Unless immediately checked, the day's routine—indeed, sometimes life itself—can get derailed. It is at such times that we need the practice of pulling the mind and the senses back. Every spiritual seeker needs this practice. It provides vital support not only to restraining the mind and the senses but also to the practices of concentration, deep faith, and forbearance.

We may want everything to go with clockwork precision, but life teaches us that it won't happen. If it is possible for anything to go wrong, it is likely that things *will* go wrong, often when we least expect it. We may want all our plans to unfold exactly the way we hope they will, but we realize quickly that life is too unpredictable for that to happen. When things don't turn out the way we thought they would, we need forbearance. This protects and preserves the rest of the "six treasures" practices. Without forbearance, life is reduced to an unending stream of distractions, eliciting frustration, disappointment, even anger.

Every practice needs focus. Nothing can be achieved with a distracted mind. It is easy to see how concentration is an inevitable requirement for the restraint of the mind and the senses. The alertness that concentration brings is an absolute must for the practices of forbearance and pulling back the mind and the senses when they go astray. Whenever faith falters, it is often due to disruption in one's focus on the ideal.

Without deep faith in the efficacy of the path we have chosen, how and why would we even engage in the practices of restraining the mind and the senses, forbearance and concentration? It is possible to say that deep faith is at the root of every spiritual practice. Without faith, practices become mechanical and lifeless. With faith, all practices come to life and can become life-transforming.

We see therefore how closely every practice in the "six treasures" is interlinked with every other, and it is for this reason that the six practices act together as if they are a single powerful practice. It is the "six treasures" which provide vital support to the other three basic practices of discernment, non-attachment, and longing for freedom.

In the following chapters, we will take a closer look at each of the practices included in the "six treasures."

CHAPTER 6

restraining the mind

The mind is a critical part of our personality. While the body has been ours only since the time we were born, the mind—the *same* mind that we have now—has been with us for life after life. In every life we get a new body, but we don't get a new mind. So it makes sense to take greater care of the mind than anything else. The mind, we are told, is a part of the problem—and, oddly enough, it is also a part of the solution. Listen to this seemingly enigmatic statement from the Amṛtabindu Upaniṣad:

> मन एव मनुष्याणां कारणं बन्धमोक्षयोः ।
>
> *Mana eva manuṣyāṇāṁ kāraṇaṁ bandha-mokṣayoḥ.*
>
> For human beings the mind alone is the cause of both bondage and freedom.

What *is* this mind that binds us but can also free us? To put it simply, the mind is a subtle part of our personality.

It is so subtle that no surgeon can find it when the body is cut open. If the body is the visible outer instrument, the mind is the invisible inner instrument (*antaḥ*=inner, *karaṇa*=instrument). When this inner instrument weighs the pros and cons of things, it is called the mind (*manas*). When it makes decisions, it is called the intellect (*buddhi*). It is often viewed as a repository (*citta*) that stores feelings, emotions, memories, and thoughts. Since it provides the sense of "I," it is also called the ego (*ahaṁkāra*). These different names merely point to the different functions of the inner instrument. While "inner instrument" is a more accurate way to describe it, it is popularly called the "mind."

Sometimes we confuse the mind with the brain, and that is a mistake. The brain is a part of the body, but the mind is not. Since the changes in the mind are sometimes reflected in the brain, it is possible to say that the mind and the brain are "connected" in some way, but the two are not identical. When the brain is damaged, it doesn't automatically imply a damaged mind, and vice versa. The changes in the brain can be objectively measured, while the changes in the mind can only be subjectively experienced. Being a part of the body, the brain dies upon the body's death, but not so the mind. When a new body is acquired—that is what "rebirth" means—the new brain becomes, so to speak, the physiological counterpart of the already existing mind.

Discernment separates good from bad, right from wrong, what is real from what is illusory—and non-attachment keeps us away from the bad, wrong and illusory. It should have been easy then to embrace what is good, right and real. But that is not how life necessarily unfolds. The mind plays a major role here, because both discernment and non-attachment occur *in* the mind. Their visible results may manifest later through action, but the process starts in the mind. The quality of discernment depends on the quality of the mind. The power of non-attachment depends on the power of the mind. The mind becomes refined and powerful only when it is disciplined.

Even the process of implementing the results of discernment and non-attachment starts in the mind. A mind is generally good at this, but there are times when it doesn't play by the rules. It gets swayed, it hesitates, it wobbles, at times it adamantly chooses to be recalcitrant. What it needs is discipline. It needs to be held in check when it tries to do what it is not supposed to do. The disciplining of the mind, restraining it when needed, is the first of the "six treasures." In Sanskrit, it is called *śama*.

What makes it difficult to discipline the mind? It is the powerful presence of mental impressions. Every action that we do and every thought we think leaves a subtle impression (*saṁskāra*) on the mind, a kind of "seed" that has the power to sprout as a desire to replay the thought or repeat the action. While mental impressions cannot force us into doing anything, they sure do influence our decision making and try to nudge us in the direction of saying yes to desires. Which desires are acted upon and which desires are left alone is decided by the will, which is generally guided by discernment and powered by non-attachment. If the mind is disciplined, it discerns well, its non-attachment is strong, and the will makes a wise and responsible choice. If the mind is erratic, its discernment lacks focus, its non-attachment is feeble, and the will becomes wayward.

A life devoted to *dharma* is what makes the mind disciplined. Dharma is a generic term in Sanskrit which stands for everything that is right and good. Dharma is what supports and holds together an individual or a community. Living according to *dharma* means upholding truth through the way we think, the way we speak, and the way we work—and doing this everywhere and at all times. Sri Ramakrishna said that

> truthfulness alone constitutes the spiritual discipline of the Kaliyuga. If people cling tenaciously to truth they ultimately realize God. Without this regard for truth, one gradually loses everything. (*Gospel*, 312)

Putting this into practice involves not only living honestly and truthfully, but also being kind and considerate while doing one's duties selflessly. In other words, moral and ethical values should guide our lives. This is spelt out beautifully in the list of moral "restraints" (*yama*) and "observances" (*niyama*) found in Patañjali's *Yoga-sūtra* (2.30, 32).

The "restraints," which are qualities essential for moral living, include the following:

1. "Nonviolence" (*ahiṁsa*) means we should abstain from injuring any being at any time in any manner. This implies absence of hatred, malice and jealousy expressed through thought, word or action.
2. "Truthfulness" (*satya*) means our words and thoughts should be in harmony between what has been seen, heard or inferred.
3. "Non-stealing" (*asteya*) means not appropriating —actually or mentally—what we are not entitled to.
4. "Dwelling in Brahman" (*brahmacarya*) means celibacy (for monastics) and chastity (for others).
5. "Non-receiving" (*aparigraha*) means not accepting things if they take away our freedom.

The "observances," which define moral conduct, include the following:

1. "Cleanliness" (*śauca*), both physical (daily shower, healthy food) and mental (freeing the mind from arrogance and greed).
2. "Contentment" (*santoṣa*) means being happy with what we have and free from hankering for what is not ours.
3. "Austerity" (*tapas*) is the ability to endure hardships and not become upset by discomfort.
4. "Self-study" (*svādhyāya*) includes both study of spiritual texts and repetition (*japa*) of mantra.
5. "Worship of God" (*īśvara-praṇidhāna*) includes

ritual worship and mental worship, as also prayer and meditation.[1]

Striving to follow these moral rules of living and conduct earnestly, day after day, year after year, is the best method of disciplining the mind. One helpful way to do this is to make a set of vows every morning, as a form of self-reminder, and try to live up to them:

1. Aware of suffering caused by the destruction of life, I vow to cultivate compassion and learn ways to prevent injury to others.
2. Aware of the harm caused by falsehood, I vow to abide by the practice of truthfulness in thought, word and deed.
3. Aware of the pain caused by exploitation, stealing and oppression, I vow to respect the property of others and protect my own as well as others' freedom.
4. Aware of damage caused by sexual misconduct, I vow to cultivate responsibility and learn ways to protect the safety and integrity of others.
5. Aware of weakness caused by greed, I vow to limit my needs to what is essential for a healthy, wholesome life.

We can also affirm our determination every morning to abide by the rules of moral conduct:

1. I am determined to maintain physical and mental cleanliness.

2. I am determined to be content with my environment and my situation in life.
3. I am determined to practice forbearance without complaint and anxiety, and learn to be in control of myself.
4. I am determined to learn the truth through study and prayer.
5. I am determined to meditate on the Supreme Being, whose existence defines mine.

Such reminders and affirmations create a strong incentive to live according to *dharma*. Creating a schedule for the daily chores also helps. The mind is a creature of habit. When we train the mind to do things in a systematic way, it instills discipline and enhances efficiency. Our workspace tends to become neat and tidy when the mind is free from clutter and confusion. A disorderly workplace often betrays a disorderly mind. That's true with our living spaces as well. When we consciously strive to be disciplined in every aspect of life, it naturally rubs off on the mind.

The first task in spiritual life is to bring the mind under control. There is no magic formula to do this other than persistent practice. Resolutely remaining focused on the ideal and keeping ourselves away from everything that distracts the mind is the practice. A simple way to accomplish this to keep the mind busy doing the things that *need* doing! For spiritual seekers, that includes their daily prayer, worship, *japa* and meditation. What could be better than doing all of these at fixed hours with faith and devotion, with regularity and sincerity? What could be better than trying to carry out all of our duties and responsibilities in the spirit of karma yoga? What could be better than trying to be mindful of every thought we think and every work we do?

None of this is easy—ah well, *life* isn't easy!—but if we strive earnestly, it is possible to control the mind. The problem is that, if we fail to control the mind, it is the mind who will control us—and we know what *that* means, for that's how our life has been, and will be, until we learn the art of taming the mind. A trained and obedient mind is an absolute delight. An indisciplined mind is an invitation to chaos and suffering.

The seemingly impossible task of taming the mind is what baffled Arjuna. He asks Krishna in the Gītā (6. 34):

> चञ्चलं हि मनः कृष्ण प्रमाथि बलवद्दृढम् ।
>
> तस्याहं निग्रहं मन्ये वायोरिव सुदुष्करम् ॥
>
> *Cañcalaṁ hi manaḥ Kṛṣṇa pramāthi balavad-dhṛḍhaṁ / Tasya-ahaṁ nigrahaṁ manye vayor-iva suduṣkaram.*
>
> O Krishna, the mind is indeed restless, turbulent, strong, unyielding. I feel that it is, like the wind, very difficult to control.

We can easily identify with Arjuna's experience. Every spiritual seeker knows what struggle with the mind feels like. Krishna acknowledges the difficulty, but also shows us how it *is* possible to restrain the mind (6. 35):

> असंशयं महाबाहो मनो दुर्निग्रहं चलम् ।
>
> अभ्यासेन तु कौन्तेय वैराग्येण च गृह्यते ॥
>
> *Asaṁśayaṁ mahābāho mano durnigrahaṁ calaṁ / Abhyāsena tu Kaunteya vairāgyeṇa ca gṛhyate.*
>
> O Son of Kunti, there is no doubt that the mind is restless and difficult to control. But it can be restrained, O mighty-armed, through practice and non-attachment.

The importance of practice and non-attachment are stressed in Patañjali's *Yoga Sutra* (I. 12) as well. The way to discipline the mind is clear. It is to live a moral and ethical life, and to let go of everything that takes me away from the spiritual ideal. When the mind is thus disciplined, it can be restrained at will.

Viewed superficially and literally, the texts sometimes seem contradictory. We read that the ultimate truth is beyond the reach of the mind and the senses (Taittirīya Upaniṣad, 2.4.1. See also Kaṭha Upaniṣad, 2.3.12) and, puzzlingly, the ultimate truth can be attained only with the help of the mind (Kaṭha Upaniṣad, 2.1.11). In his commentary, Śrī Śaṅkarācārya explains that while the truth is indeed beyond the mind's reach, it can be attained "by a purified mind." Sri Ramakrishna put it this way: "It is God who dwells within as the pure mind and pure intelligence" (*Gospel,* 853).

There is symbiosis between the practices of discernment, non-attachment, and restraining the mind. On one hand, discernment leads to non-attachment and, together, they prepare us for the practice of restraining the mind. On the other hand, a mind that is disciplined deepens discernment and strengthens non-attachment. These practices depend on one another and each fulfills the others.

CHAPTER 7

restraining the senses

Most of us have no idea how many processes are vigorously at work inside a computer to make it easy for us to write or read a text, to watch a video, or to listen to music. A software code may look like total gibberish to the untrained eye, but thanks to those apparently nonsensical set of numbers, letters and symbols, and the hardware that complements them, even dummies like us can understand what we get to see on our screens. Something similar happens when the world appears on the screens of our minds. There is a lot going on below the surface. Really a lot!

What the senses bring to the mind are an incredible variety of sensations of sight, sound, smell, taste, and touch. The moment the sensations come in, they are at once compared to the database in the mind and decoded. Each sensation is assigned a meaning with a corresponding idea and word. The incoming information gathered by the senses then seems to coalesce magically into a recognizable world, bringing to life what feels like a three-dimensional reality with all its colors and flavors, sights and sounds—and *that* is what we see on the mind's screen. All of this happens instantaneously.

As Swami Vivekananda wrote (CW, 9. 297): "Something —'x'—acts on the brain through the nerves, the reaction is this world." He elaborated on this in a lecture he delivered in Lahore (presently in Pakistan) on November 12, 1897:

> Suppose we represent the external world by "x," what we really know is "x" plus mind, and this mind-element is so great that it has covered the whole of that "x" which has remained unknown and unknowable throughout; and, therefore, if there is an external world, it is always unknown and unknowable. What we know of it is as it is moulded, formed, fashioned by our own mind. (CW, 3. 403)[1]

It is clear that we don't really see the world, we only see the interpreted version of the incoming sensations. It feels like a colossal cosmic conspiracy meant to delude us into believing in the existence of the world as we see it. What is really out there, if anything at all, is something we may never know.

It is the outward movement of the senses that starts the ball rolling. It doesn't take too long to find ourselves getting embroiled in the world, an involvement that makes our life inseparable from stress and strain, pain and suffering. The problem begins with the senses going out. That's the *only* thing the senses do! They go out, not in, so outside is all that we see, not inside. It is almost as if the senses are deliberately designed with this deficiency. Listen to the words of the Kaṭha Upaniṣad (2.1.1):

> पराञ्चि खानि व्यतृणत् स्वयम्भूस्तस्मात्पराङ्पश्यति नान्तरात्मन् ।
>
> *parāñci khāni vyatṛṇat svayambhūs-tasmāt parāṅ-paśyati na antar-ātman.*
>
> The self-existent [Supreme Being] destroyed the senses by creating them with outgoing tendencies. That is why people see only what is outside, not the inner self.

Even one of the senses—what to speak of *five*—is enough to bring about destruction. Attracted to the sound of a mimicked deer call, a deer is lured by hunters. Attracted to touch and moving in tightly knit groups, elephants often walk into pit traps. Attracted to the light of a flame, a moth is burnt to death. Attracted to taste, a fish bites the bait. Attracted to smell, a bee dies by foraging on the nectar of toxic plants. Śrī Śaṅkarācārya's *Vivekacūḍāmaṇi*, 76, points this out in a powerful verse:

> शब्दादिभिः पञ्चभिरेव पञ्च पञ्चत्वमापुः स्वगुणेन बद्धाः ।
>
> कुरङ्ग-मातङ्ग-पतङ्ग-मीन-भृङ्गा नरः पञ्चभिरञ्चितः किम् ॥
>
> *Śabdādibhiḥ pañcabhir-eva pañca pañcatvam-āpuḥ svaguṇena baddhāḥ; / Kuraṅga-mātaṅga-pataṅga-mīna-bhṛngāḥ naraḥ pañcabhir-añcitaḥ kim.*

> The attraction to even one of these five sense objects, such as sound etc., becomes the cause of death to a deer, an elephant, a moth, a fish, and a bee. What, then, to speak of the human being who is attracted to all of these five!

This is at once a sobering and frightening realization. The senses are at present a source of our happiness but they also bring sorrow and suffering. That is what the "outside" does to us. What about the "inside"? Inside is where the self is, the real me. To see the inner self I have to stop looking outside—and the only way to do that is to shut the outgoing senses, which is by no means easy. It needs a courageous, determined person to do this. The Kaṭha Upaniṣad (2.1.1) goes on to say:

> कश्चिद्धीरः प्रत्यगात्मानमैक्षदावृत्तचक्षुरमृतत्वमिच्छन् ।
>
> *Kaścit dhiraḥ pratyag-ātmānam aikṣat āvṛtta-cakṣuḥ amṛtattvam icchan.*
>
> Seeking immortality, a rare discerning person shuts the senses and beholds the inner self.

Obviously, the difficult part is to shut the senses. How can we stop the chronically outgoing senses from going out? One way is to try to shut the door on them, at least as best we can. That is what we try to do while praying and meditating. We close our eyes, we don't eat, we try to find a place free from noise and any offensive odor, and we don't wear skin-tight clothes. We can't close the senses totally but even a partial covering helps. What cannot be shut down as easily is the mind, hence the importance of having the mind under control, the practice known as *śama,* which we discussed in the last chapter.

While it makes sense to stop feeding the senses as far as it is possible during prayer and meditation, we obviously cannot do that all the time for the simple reason that it is not possible to do so, but even if it were, what would be the point of living if the senses are shut down all the time? The senses are troublesome all right, but is there anything we can do about it? Since we cannot change their basic nature, let us at least learn from the experiences they bring us.

The vital question is: can I allow the senses to do what they do while still retaining control over them? The answer is yes. I only have to train the senses properly through the practice of discernment and non-attachment. This should normally free me from suffering, but that is not what happens, because *life* happens. Past habits force me to go back to thinking and doing the way I have done countless times before to my own detriment and sorrow.

Only when an experience is especially traumatic or challenging does it leave behind a deep enough impression that will prevent me from repeating the action. If I have suffered from poison ivy, I shall instinctively keep away from areas that have more of them. If looking directly at the sun has damaged my eyes, I will never again attempt to do that. If I am allergic to certain foods, then I'll avoid eating them. With the exception of such situations, our senses take in everything quite indiscriminately. They have no inbuilt filters and that's a problem.

It is helpful to remember the evocative chariot imagery presented in the Kaṭha Upaniṣad (1.3.3-9). The body (*śarīra*) is the chariot and the Ātman is the master. The intellect (*buddhi*) is the charioteer, the mind (*manas*) is the reins, and the senses (*indriya*) are the horses galloping on the path of this world, which is filled with varied objects of all kinds. To reach the destination quickly and safely, it is vital that the charioteer remains alert, holding the reins tightly (*śama*) and controlling the horses (*dama*), so they don't go berserk but remain on the path. What we need is a charioteer who is vigilant, determined and in control—and that is what makes restraining the senses easier. This practice is the second of the "six treasures" and is known as *dama*.

Restraining the senses is like breaking a horse, but not doing it too harshly. Consider the practice of fasting. An occasional fast can be a powerful way to ascertain my control over the body and the senses. We know that the body needs to be fed and, every few hours, it demands food. The sense of taste hungers for what is delicious, the sense of smell looks for what is appetizing. It is generally a good idea to provide them what they need, but it is also good to now and then say "no" to them, just to let them know who calls the shots. That is what fasting really is. It also applies to the "food" I provide the mind from mindless surfing of the internet or other pastimes that entertain but don't teach. Fasting saves physical and mental energy, which then can be used for better things. Fasting disciplines the body and the senses, and affirms my freedom. Fasting shouldn't be overdone. The point is not to torture myself but to bring some order to my life.

The two practices—restraining the mind and restraining the senses—are clearly connected and interdependent. They support and enhance each other. A disciplined mind helps the process of restraining the senses, and the restrained senses make controlling the mind easier. We might as well think of the two practices as one composite practice.

We have so far seen two of the "six treasures"—namely, restraining the mind and restraining the senses. The third is the practice of pulling the mind and the senses back if they manage to slip away in spite of the restraints. That is what we will turn to in the next chapter.

CHAPTER 8

pulling back

Restraining a restless dog can be challenging, but it is considerably more challenging to get hold of the dog after he's managed to free himself from the leash. That is the difference between *restraining* the mind and the senses, and *pulling* them back when they break free. The practice of pulling back (*uparati*) is the third of the "six treasures."

Every thought we think and every action we do leaves a subtle impression on the mind. These impressions reside in the mental basement, so to speak. That is why we are not conscious of them all the time, except when they rise up in the form of desires in order to replicate the experience of the original thought or action. When we act upon those desires, we create more impressions, which later produce even more desires. It is a loop that gets progressively more vicious. In a talk given in New York on December 18, 1895, Swami Vivekananda said:

> Most of our time is spent in thinking about sense objects, things which we have seen, or we have heard, which we shall see or shall hear, things which we have eaten, or are eating, or shall eat, places where we have lived, and so on. We think of them or talk of them most of our time. One who wishes to be a Vedānta student must give up this habit. (CW, 1. 406)

The practice of non-attachment follows discernment and helps the subsequent practices of restraining the mind and the senses. The power of all of these practices is considerable, but it sometimes fails to keep the mind and the senses in check, such is the force of the impressions gathered through God-knows-how-many lives. When we are not attentive, the mind and the senses manage to slip away and run toward everything they find attractive.

Left on their own, the senses are programmed to engage with the world. The work of the senses can be useful and productive when done intentionally and with a specific purpose. After all, without the mind and the senses we would know nothing about the world. But the mind and the senses are at their best only when they are monitored and controlled. Uparati consists in pulling the mind back whenever it breaks free from its restraints and pulling the senses back every time they run any which way.

Always remaining alert, never allowing our thinking and doing to be mechanical, is the key to understanding and knowledge (*see* Kena Upaniṣad, 2. 4). When we are mindful, everything is just as it should be. When we are not, unexpected and unwanted things happen.

There is one thing we all living beings share in common, and that is—we don't want to suffer. We don't like being miserable. We don't want to put ourselves in situations that will bring us pain. Can we use this simple fact to make it easier to pull the mind and the senses back? That is what the sage Patañjali seems to suggest in his *Yoga-sūtra* (2. 33):

> वितर्कबाधने प्रतिपक्षभावनम् ।
>
> *Vitarka-bādhane pratipakṣa-bhāvanam.*
>
> To obstruct inimical thoughts, contrary thoughts should be raised.

How do we do this? One way is to remind ourselves of the suffering our "inimical thoughts" and consequent actions might bring upon us. Whatever takes us away from the spiritual ideal can only result in greater sorrow and suffering sooner or later. Raising this "contrary thought" and remaining vigilant always, the mind and the senses learn to avoid what is harmful and to embrace what is healthy. If certain things, places or people evoke feelings of hatred, anger or such other negativities, I must keep away from them as far as possible, reminding myself of the harm such feelings do to my spiritual life.

Swami Vivekananda suggests an alternative way to raise "contrary thoughts":

> For instance, when a big wave of anger has come into the mind, how are we to control that? Just by raising an

> opposing wave. Think of love. Sometimes a mother is very angry with her husband, and while in that state, the baby comes in, and she kisses the baby; the old wave dies out and a new wave arises, love for the child. That suppresses the other one. Love is opposite to anger. (CW, I. 261)

It may not be easy to raise the thought of love when we are in a fit of anger, but making an effort can be rewarding. One practice that works like magic is to force ourselves to smile whenever overcome by negative feelings, even boredom. The relaxed muscles of a smiling face make it virtually impossible to frown at the same time. The expression on the face of the Buddha in meditation or of Ramakrishna in samādhi can be ours through practice. Granted, we may not be able to wear it as naturally as Buddha or Ramakrishna did, but even then it works! If we practice it often and consistently, it may even become our default expression, which will also help when we sit down to meditate.

Setting boundaries and making rules for ourselves is a good practice. When we are mindful, we generally stick by our rules. When we lose focus, the instinctive part of our personality takes over. If we have, for instance, decided to curb our screen time and stay away from the phone, computer, television, or games console at certain hours of the day, we need to use all of our will-power to abide by that discipline. If and when we mechanically reach out to pick up our devices when we shouldn't, the practice of pulling back comes into play. Maintaining discipline in one's personal life is essential for efficiency in everything we do.

The practice of pulling back looks very similar to the practice of non-attachment. How do we distinguish between the two? One important distinction is that pulling back occurs only from things that are tangible, those within the reach of the senses, whereas the practice of non-attachment also includes things that are not immediately visible, such as the intense but ephemeral pleasures of heaven. Another distinction is that non-attachment is the natural result of discernment and is, as it were, the first line of defense, whereas the practice of pulling back is a kind of backup when the practices of restraining the mind and the senses fail for whatever reason.

The following are among the things we can do to practice pulling back when necessary:

1. To minimize the need for pulling back, we have to remain mindful of what we think, what we say, what we do—and not allow our thoughts, words and actions to become mechanical. The key is self-discipline.
2. When restraint fails, we must try to remind ourselves of the harm or pain and sorrow our thinking or doing at the time will cause us (and possibly others), which is something none of us wants.
3. Another things we can do in difficult situations is to consciously neutralize harmful thought and

> actions by intentionally raising healthy thoughts in the mind, so hatred can be conquered through love, enmity through friendship, violence through peace and harmony.

Next among the "six treasures" is the practice of forbearance, to which we now turn in the next chapter.

CHAPTER 9

forbearance

Sooner or later we all realize that not everything in life happens the way we hope it will. Not every plan is going to succeed, not every situation is going to be favorable, not every person is going to be agreeable. Some, yes; most, if we are lucky; but never all. Life is too complicated, the world is too complex, and hardly anything here is predictable. The universe is too big and its forces are too powerful to manipulate. No matter how we see ourselves, in the larger picture we are nobodies and obviously we are powerless to change the way the world-machine works.

In spite of our best efforts, when things go wrong—as they sometimes will—we can choose to rave and rant, or to blast and blame, or to grieve and gripe. But there is also one more option. If we haven't learnt this already, life will teach us that when there is no obvious cure, the best option is to learn to endure, and to do it calmly, even cheerfully. Holy Mother Sri Sarada Devi's teaching is both practical and profound: "One who forbears, survives. One who doesn't forbear is destroyed." The practice of forbearance (*titikṣā*) is the fourth among the "six treasures."

In a talk given in New York on December 18, 1895, Swami Vivekananda spoke of forbearance as a practice that is "the most difficult of all" (CW, 1. 406). Śrī Śaṅkarācārya defines the practice succinctly in his *Vivekacūḍāmaṇi,* 24:

> सहनं सर्वदुःखानामप्रतीकारपूर्वकम् ।
>
> चिन्ताविलापरहितं सा तितिक्षा निगद्यते ॥
>
> *Sahanaṁ sarva-duḥkhānām apratikāra-pūrvakam, / Cintā-vilāpa-rahitaṁ sā titikṣā nigadyate.*
>
> Bearing all suffering without resistance, without anxiety and without grumbling is called forbearance.

Even if we are super careful and vigilant, we still cannot avoid suffering. It will sneak into our lives one way or another. How shall we respond to it? The best way is to do it without resistance, without anxiety, and without grumbling.

That is what Arjuna did not do. When faced with the prospect of fighting his own kith and kin, Arjuna resisted, he became anxious, he bemoaned his situation. He was confused. To calm him down and to bring clarity to his mind, Krishna's immediate response was to reiterate the obvious. Life is filled with ups and downs, the pleasant and the unpleasant. All experience of pain and pleasure is transitory. Krishna's advice to Arjuna: "Practice forbearance" (Gītā, 2. 14).

When we begin the practice, we quickly realize how difficult it is. But when we manage to do it well, we become free from distractions and can focus the mind on what *really* matters. It might seem as if the practice of forbearance is necessitated by our helplessness, but we eventually discover that it is in fact "the highest expression of freedom" (CW, 1. 67).

Without resistance

It is one thing to not resist because we are incapable of doing so, but quite another to not resist in spite of having the power, the ability, and the opportunity to do so. Nonresistance does not become a virtue if it springs from weakness or lack of opportunity to retaliate.[1] Even fantasizing about retaliation is a kind of inner resistance. It is a form of weakness and not real forbearance.

Swami Vivekananda said that forbearance is nothing less than practicing "resist not evil." This is how he explained it:

> We may not resist an evil, but at the same time we may feel very miserable. Others may say very harsh things to me, and I may not outwardly hate them for it, may not answer them back, and may restrain myself from apparently getting angry, but anger and hatred may be in my mind, and I may feel very badly towards them. That is not non-resistance! I should be without any feeling of

> hatred or anger, without any thought of resistance. My mind must be as calm as if nothing had happened. And only when I have got to that state, have I attained to non-resistance, and not before. (CW, 1. 406)

How difficult it is to not react! Reacting to whatever is happening around us seems to be a most natural thing to do. But no reaction is what non-resistance is all about. To react is easy, to *not* react is tough. Listen to Vivekananda's words:

> As soon as we react, we become slaves. A man blames me, and I immediately react in the form of anger. A little vibration which he created made me a slave. So we have to demonstrate our freedom. (CW, 5. 290)

It may so happen that I have to endure even more suffering because I did not react and resist. Even then I should not feel any regret for not resisting. When my mind reaches such a state, then I have attained to real forbearance (CW, 1. 406). Not reacting needs outstanding courage:

> It is easy to strike a blow, but tremendously hard to stay the hand, stand still, and say, "In Thee, O Lord, I take refuge," and then wait for Him to act. (CW 7. 31)

Understood as a form of non-resistance, is forbearance practical? Probably not for most of us. If everyone decides to practice non-resistance, the social fabric will come tumbling down. The wicked will do terrible things with impunity and there will be no such thing as justice. Fortunately, the world is never short of forces trying to fight for justice in the face of injustice. The world does need people to react and there will always be those who react and resist.

While resistance can be good and at times even necessary, it cannot be denied that it can—and often does—lead to greater suffering, not less. That is why the world also needs at least a few souls strong enough to practice non-resistance in spite of provocation. There are always some in every generation. To practice non-resistance is not easy by any measure, but that is the ideal.

Without anxiety

Suffering is painful in itself, but what adds to the pain is the anxiety regarding it—how long will I have to suffer? How often do I have to suffer like this? Will it get worse? And also: what have I done to deserve this? Life is unfair! Anxiety makes suffering worse.

How do I overcome anxiety? A devotee reasons this way: everything happens through God's will. If I am suffering now, that is what God wants for me. God loves me, so this must be for my good, even if I have no idea what good will be accomplished by my suffering. The devotee's faith in God and surrender to the divine will overcome the natural impulse to be anxious, to resist, to retaliate. They also fill the devotee with strength that lightens the burden and makes it easier to endure the suffering with patience. While suffering is no picnic when it's happening, when we look back at it days or months or years later, we almost always smile at the experience, even discover that in an odd sort of way it turned things around for us. If we are going to smile at it sometime in the future, we may as well begin now!

Another way to think about suffering is through the lens of the karma theory, which is based on the principles of justice and responsibility. Nothing happens without a reason. Every effect can be traced back to a cause. If I am suffering, I have contributed to it in some way, even if I do not remember how and when I did that. Trying to understand my own suffering—not someone else's—through the karma-lens is a better option than trying to find a scapegoat to blame for my woes.

Karma is also empowering, because I know that it is me, and no one else, who can make me happy or make me miserable. Swami Vivekananda's words come to mind:

> Stand up, be bold, be strong. Take the whole responsibility on your own shoulders, and know that you are the creator of your own destiny. All the strength and succor you want is within yourselves. Therefore, make your own future. (CW, 2. 225)

If I change, my experience also changes. Changing myself is a lot easier than making futile attempts to change others. Further, blaming others compounds the suffering. Taking responsibility lessens it.

Without grumbling

No one knows why people grumble. It does no good to anyone. Far from improving a situation, grumbling makes it worse. "To the grumbler, all duties are distasteful," said Swami Vivekananda. "Nothing will ever satisfy such people, and their whole life is doomed to prove a failure" (CW, 1. 71). Strong words, these.

Grumbling is also a colossal waste of energy and it makes the grumbler's life miserable, increasing the suffering, not lessening it. It's a mystery why it is so difficult to learn what is absurdly obvious—that the less we grumble, the happier we are. Deciding resolutely to never grumble is an extremely beneficial practice.

To summarize—suffering is inevitable and unavoidable in life. The best way to respond to it is by being calm, even managing to smile (if I am up to it), but certainly doing this without resistance, without anxiety and without grumbling. The practice of forbearance accumulates enormous inner power. All I need to do then is to direct this power toward the pursuit of my spiritual goal.

Forbearance may be the most difficult practice, but if I can pull it off, I'll taste true happiness.

CHAPTER 10

concentration

The Sanskrit word *samādhāna* has many connotations. What comes immediately to mind is "satisfaction" or "contentment," which is how the word is popularly understood in some Indian languages. If we examine how the word is derived, we get a clearer picture. It is a combination of two terms, "proper" (*samyak*) and "placing" (*ādhāna*). Placing the mind properly on any activity—meaning with total attention—not only is an efficient way to do things but it also brings considerable satisfaction. The practice of placing the mind properly—in short, concentration (*samādhāna*) —is the fifth of the "six treasures."

Where is the mind concentrated in the practice of Vedānta? Śaṅkarācārya makes that clear in his definition of the term (*Vivekacūḍāmaṇi*, 26):

सम्यगास्थापनं बुद्धेः शुद्धे ब्रह्मणि सर्वदा ।

तत्समाधानमित्युक्तं न तु चित्तस्य लालनम् ।

samyag-āsthāpanaṁ buddheḥ śuddhe brahmaṇi sarvadā, /
Tat samādhānam-iti-uktam na tu cittasya lālanam.

Concentration does not mean pampering the mind but directing it fully toward the pure Brahman.

The definition has a note of warning. Every concentrated activity brings intellectual or emotional satisfaction, or both, and results in contentment. But if contentment is all that we seek, then that would be nothing more than "pampering the mind." For concentration to become a spiritual practice, the mind needs to be focused on the highest ideal. In Vedānta, the ideal is Consciousness-itself unattached to any object, signified by the term Brahman (lit. "vast, infinite"). The qualifier "pure" in the verse denotes that Brahman is unique and nondual, uncontaminated by the existence of anything else.

As an ideal, Brahman often feels too abstract. We may find Brahman too impersonal. The spiritual ideal almost always becomes more real, more tangible, more accessible, when it is seen in personal terms, clothed in the language of form and qualities. This personal aspect of the Divine may *appear* different, but it is not really different from Brahman. It is the same reality seen through the lens of form and qualities. When the lens melts away, as it eventually does, the seeming difference between the form and the formless, the personal and the impersonal, disappears too. In truth, Brahman is neither personal nor impersonal but beyond them both.

Though not a spiritual goal in itself, contentment is nevertheless a helpful state of mind for the practice of concentration. If the mind is filled with despondency or too much exuberance, it becomes unfit for spiritual practice. Not for nothing did Swami Vivekananda say:

> Despondency is not religion, whatever else it may be. By being pleasant always and smiling, it takes you nearer to God, nearer than any prayer. ... At the same time you must avoid excessive merriment. A mind in that state never becomes calm; it becomes fickle. Excessive merriment will always be followed by sorrow. Tears and laughter are near kin. People so often run from one extreme to the other. Let the mind be cheerful, but calm. Never let it run into excesses, because every excess will be followed by a reaction. (CW, 4. 11)

Can we find the ideal middle ground, neither wallowing in despair nor brimming with excitement, but simply dwelling in serenity? For concentration to succeed, it is essential that the mind remain alert, contented and cheerful, but without reacting to every stupid stimulus, internal or external.

What does the practice of concentration do? Three things, all very important. First, it helps me gain knowledge. As Swami Vivekananda pointed out:

> The world is ready to give up its secrets if we only know how to knock, how to give it the necessary blow. The

> strength and force of the blow come through concentration. (CW 1. 130-31).

The human mind is much more powerful than we think. The more concentrated the mind becomes, the more of its power becomes manifest, leading to greater and deeper knowledge. Ignorance of our true nature is at the root of all our problems—so knowledge of who we really are is what we absolutely need.[1]

The second benefit of concentration is that it increases the power of assimilation which, for spiritual seekers, shortens the time for gaining knowledge and attaining illumination. It is as if the illumined soul manages to live in a single lifetime the millions of years of the gently evolving life of entire humanity.[2] The more concentrated the mind is, the more transparent it becomes and reveals the truth fully and clearly.

Improving the efficiency and quality of our work is the third benefit of the practice. This is something most of us will have experienced in our own lives. There are times when we lose ourselves in the work, so fully immersed we are in it, so focused and concentrated, that when the work is over, we discover to our great joy that the quality of the work is immensely better than if we had done the same work in an egoistic way, anxious about the results or hankering for recognition.

The practice of concentration thus leads to knowledge, increases the power of assimilation, accelerates spiritual progress, and improves the quality of work. Tremendous as these benefits are, the difficulties in concentrating the mind are tremendous as well.

That is why merely a desire to concentrate is never enough for success in the practice. We also need love—real love. Concentration becomes easy, natural and effortless when there is love in the heart. The quality of my meditation, and my success in it, are directly related to how much I love my chosen ideal (*iṣṭa-devatā*). Bereft of love, the practice becomes mechanical, dry and ultimately fruitless.

Recognizing the importance of the practice is another factor that makes a big difference. When I am trying to concentrate, do I believe that my meditation practice is important enough for me to set aside all other priorities at least for a time? Am I convinced that the practice is worth the time and energy that I am investing into it? The presence of what we call distractions is nothing but things that the mind considers *more* important than what I am trying to do in meditation. If my mind routinely chooses to ignore me and goes its own way—that is a huge problem.

The hurdles to concentration begin to disappear when I am able to get control over my mind and the senses. Which is why restraint of the mind and the senses is so vital for good concentration. When the mind and the senses are disciplined, a life dedicated to ethical values becomes a natural way to live. Supported by a strong motivation, which is provided by the power of love toward the ideal, distractions gradually disappear and concentration is no longer a challenge. Everything is done with a mind that is focused, not with strenuous effort but because of the mind's natural disposition.

Once we taste the utter joy and freedom of living with a mind that is free to attach itself to anything totally and unreservedly—which is what concentration is—but also detach itself completely when the job is done, it is impossible to go back to our old ways of life.

CHAPTER 11

deep faith

Faith plays a much bigger role in our lives than we imagine. Life would come to a standstill without faith. Referring to religions as "faiths" and restricting the word to religious matters has led to ignoring how pervasive faith is in our daily lives. We use public transportation (with faith that whoever is flying our plane or driving our bus is alert and careful), we eat in restaurants (with faith that the food won't make us sick), we take elevators (with faith that they won't crash), we make investments (with faith that they will provide good returns). We may think that all of these are reasonable things to do, and they are, but none of us knows in advance how they'll turn out. We do them anyway. It is faith and hope that power our actions, and reason often plays only a secondary role.

But faith can be shaken or even lost due to a bad experience, especially a traumatic one. This happens often in varied contexts throughout our lives. There is, however, something else which looks like faith but, once it arrives, it is never shaken and never lost. Think of it as a profound kind of faith, call it "deep faith" if you like. In Sanskrit it is called *śraddhā*. To understand *śraddhā,* the sixth among the "six treasures," let us turn to Śrī Śaṅkarācārya in his *Vivekacūḍāmaṇi,* 25:

> शास्त्रस्य गुरुवाक्यस्य सत्यबुध्यवधारणम् ।
>
> सा श्रद्धा कथिता सद्भिर्यया वस्तूपलभ्यते ॥
>
> *Śāstrasya guru-vākyasya satya-buddhi-ava-dhāraṇam, / Sā śraddhā kathitā sadbhiḥ yayā vastu-upalabhyate.*
>
> The wise say that deep faith, by means of which the Real is attained, means accepting as authentic the words of the scripture and of one's teacher.

The definition unequivocally affirms that deep faith is a means to attaining the Real, which is how Brahman or God is sometimes referred to. The Gītā (4. 39) emphasizes this as well:

> श्रद्धावान् लभते ज्ञानं तत्परः संयतेन्द्रियः ।
>
> *śraddhāvān labhate jñānaṁ tat paraḥ saṁyata-indriyaḥ.*
>
> The person of deep faith, who is devoted and has controlled the senses, attains [the highest] knowledge.

The measure of deep faith determines the spiritual potential in a person's heart (Gītā, 17. 3). Deep faith is often thought of as the most vital requirement to even begin the spiritual quest.

Why is it so important to accept as authentic the words of the scripture and one's teacher? It is important because, without deep faith in their authenticity, why would I even want to study the scripture or follow the teacher? Would I really give my all to spiritual life or invest myself fully into it if I wasn't sure that it would lead me to God? The efforts of a cynical, doubting mind inevitably fall short. A half-hearted attempt seldom gives us the success we seek.

Accepting the scripture and the teacher as authentic does not mean following them blindly. Gullibility is no virtue in spiritual life, but nor is cynicism. It is possible to be alert so we are never taken for a ride and, at the same time, open to learning and growing. At the very least, it means to accept the teaching as a working hypothesis that we can verify through our own experience—and to reserve the right to reject it if it doesn't work for us. In the case of Vedānta, the teaching has been around for centuries. It has transformed lives for the better and led earnest seekers to spiritual enlightenment. That makes it much easier to accept the teaching and the practice as authentic.

But deep faith is never really the result of a deliberative process. It is seldom something that we have to make a decision about. The arrival of deep faith in the heart happens on its own. For some, it is gentle, so gradual that they may not even realize it when it happens. For others, it can be an aha! moment and feel like a miracle. We don't really get to choose how and when deep faith arrives and envelops our life. But when it does, life changes for us. Accepting the scripture and the teacher then feels natural and effortless.

Deep faith is not a function of the intellect or of emotions. It is not an idea or a feeling. Deep faith is a mysterious and powerful force dwelling deep within us. It is something in the gut, so to speak, that says, "yes, it's true"—about God, the scripture and the teacher. The power embedded in deep faith is divine in nature and is present in all beings:

> या देवी सर्वभूतेषु श्रद्धारूपेण संस्थिता ।
>
> नमस्तस्यै, नमस्तस्यै, नमस्तस्यै, नमो नमः ॥
>
> *Yā devī sarva-bhuteṣu śraddhā-rūpeṇa saṁsthitā, / Namas-tasyai, namas-tasyai, namas-tasyai, namo namaḥ.*
>
> Salutations again and again to the Divine Mother that abides in all beings in the form of deep faith. (*Durgā Saptaśati*, 5. 50-52)

It is deep faith that generates both the motivation and the energy to pursue truth. We get a glimpse of it in the life of Naciketā when "deep faith entered into him" (Kaṭha Upaniṣad, 1.1.2) and no temptations could distract him (1.1.23-25) from his single-minded quest to solve the mystery of death and beyond. At the end of the teaching, Naciketā became "free from impurities and death and attained Brahman" (2.3.18).

It is difficult to explain to others, especially to skeptics, the phenomenon of deep faith. In the beginning we have no personal experience of God. Nor do we have any objective evidence to convince others. Quoting from a scripture is useless if the other person doesn't see the text as worthy of total trust. The only way deep faith can be shared is through the power of one's own life. When deep faith transforms us into better versions of ourselves, those who notice the change can clearly see the immense power of faith—and that can encourage them to take it more seriously than they did before. There are, of course, countless examples in history of extraordinary people of deep faith and their spiritual attainments, but it may not mean much to a skeptic. To a doubting mind, everything is suspect, only the doubt is real.

But if deep faith arrives on its own, do I have to just keep waiting for its arrival? Is there anything I can do to make it come sooner? There are at least two things within my control.

Although it feels as if deep faith appears out of nowhere, it really is—as we have seen— already present in every heart. I remain unaware of it because I am too preoccupied with matters of this world that somehow feel more important, more urgent, more pressing. If there is anything at all beyond this world, I feel that it can wait, since it is hidden anyway in the dark cloud of the unknown, invisible future. The problem is that I don't know when the cloud will disperse, the seemingly distant future will suddenly become the immediate present, and I'll find myself near the gaping mouth of death approaching rapidly to swallow me. It may be too late then to do anything.

Now is the time to do whatever needs to be done. Wherever I am now is the place where the process must begin. There is no time like now. There is no place like here. Even while I am busy with my life, I should be aware that all of the things, no matter how important and urgent they seem, are going to disappear when I die. My last moment can come at *any* time, probably sooner than I imagine. What then? What's next for me? Do I step into the unknown darkness, terrified and unsure—or do I want to step into the divine effulgence, breathing the fresh air of freedom with joy in my heart? Even a little bit of foresight makes us aware of the urgency of the spiritual quest and that helps in removing complacency, which is a major obstacle to deep faith.

Another obstacle is the crust of cynicism that tends to cover the mind as I navigate my way through life. Bitterness, anger, frustration, the sense of being cheated, or of being deprived of what I deserve, or of being scalded by the seeming injustices around me—all of this is enough to make me feel so hopeless and cynical that I may no longer believe that goodness and honor, kindness and love, do exist. It is true that the world has an ugly side and that some people can be awful, but it is important to remind myself that there are also people who are truly good, sincere, honest, trustworthy.

Trying to see goodness even in the midst of a hopeless situation is in itself a powerful, even if difficult, practice.

We have to be careful not to allow ourselves to be cheated or exploited or abused. We need to be strong, but we also need to trust that essentially human beings are good. If we look deeply, it is not too difficult to find the light of hope even in the darkness of a dire situation. If we are looking for goodness, we'll find it. If we are looking for love, we'll find that too.

Sooner or later we all find what we are looking for. It's up to us to look for the right things in the right places. That is the only way to not be infected by negativity and cynicism, despondency and depression. It is possible to live peacefully and happily, without hurting others or allowing others to hurt us. If we can manage to remain positive, no matter what, then we succeed in removing another layer that covers the deep faith already present in our hearts.

In this way, being good ourselves and striving to see goodness everywhere and in everyone, remaining alert and hopeful but never taking life for granted, hastens the emergence of deep faith. What does it do when it arrives? A lot really.

Deep faith brings about a profound change, such as deep inner stability, calmness and hope. The faith is "deep" but without the combativeness we see in a fanatic. A person with deep faith is the *opposite* of a fanatic, because deep faith brings enormous breadth of vision, the spirit of understanding and acceptance. When deep faith engages with the intellect, it brings clarity and conviction. When deep faith engages with the heart, it becomes filled with devotion to God or the spiritual ideal. When deep faith engages with the will, it works in two ways. Internally, it spurs deeper reflection; externally, it converts work into worship.

Deep faith is at the root of every spiritual discipline, whether it takes the form of philosophical inquiry or love for God or contemplation or selfless service, or a combination of two or more or all of these. Without deep faith, none of these is possible. With deep faith, nothing is impossible. Deep faith galvanizes us. It kickstarts our spiritual life.

When followed up by sustained practice, deep faith matures into a direct encounter with the Divine. When we started out, it was deep faith that held our hand and it was spiritual practice that guided us through the darkness of ignorance. Deep faith and dedicated practice, each supporting the other, take us beyond the "doing" part of spirituality to "being" the spirit. This occurs through spiritual absorption (*samādhi*), when the fog clears and we encounter the Divine—inside, outside, above, below, everywhere. The "I" disappears and the Divine alone remains. We have reached the end of the tunnel and emerged into the bright sunshine of wisdom and freedom. Deep faith has done its job. It now disappears as mysteriously as it once appeared. It's no longer needed.

Nothing is needed any more. We need what we lack. When we lack nothing, we need nothing. Needs are a sign of bondage. Freedom implies no needs, no duties, no limitations. Nothing more needs to be done other than just being. Being our true selves. Awake, peaceful, happy. Just being who we are, unbounded by time and space, missing nothing and no one, being everything and everyone.

It all begins with deep faith.

CHAPTER 12

longing for freedom

Longing for freedom is traditionally listed last among the Four Basic Practices, but it should really top the list. After all, unless there is longing for spiritual freedom (*mokṣa*), why would anyone take the trouble to do any spiritual practice? There is an ancient saying in India, “Even a fool doesn’t do anything without a motive.”

The longing for freedom provides the reason, the motivation, the purpose which makes all Vedānta practices meaningful. In order to want freedom, we should first of all recognize that presently we are not free. The need for freedom won’t make any sense if we don’t feel our bondage or if we feel that we are already free. Śaṅkarācārya’s definition of the longing for freedom points to both the nature of the bondage and the way to freedom.

अहंकारादिदेहान्तान् बन्धानज्ञानकल्पितान् ।
स्वस्वरूपावबोधेन भोक्तुमिच्छा मुमुक्षुता ॥

Ahaṁkārādi-dehāntān bandhān ajñāna-kalpitān, / Sva-svarūpa-avabodhena bhoktum icchā mumukṣutā.

The longing for freedom is the desire to be free from the bondage of ignorance—meaning, the body and the ego, etc.—by knowing one's own true nature. (*Vivekacūḍāmaṇi*, 27)

IF WE ARE HONEST, we can easily see how little we know about anything. My knowledge about "things" may vary, but what about my knowledge about myself? I probably feel I already know who I am, but what if I am wrong? I am wrong about many things in life. This could be one of them. It is possible that I am *not* who I think I am. My ignorance about myself shows up through "the body and the ego, etc."

According to Vedānta, my true nature is pure and perfect. I am infinite, eternal and free. Obviously that is not how I see myself—and *that* is because of my ignorance. It looks like I am in the grip of a strange kind of amnesia. I have no idea how or why this happened. I am told that the forgetfulness of my true identity has made it possible for me to project a false perception of myself as a human being with a body.

Besides my body, which is visible to me and to others, there is also a part of me which is subtle and hidden from the world. That is "the ego, etc" part, which is called the "inner instrument." As we saw before, depending on its multiple functions, it is variously characterized as the ego, the intellect, the mind, the storehouse of thoughts, memories and tendencies. The inner instrument is popularly known as simply the mind, which makes it logical and easy to see the body as the *outer* instrument. Both these "instruments"—body and mind—are so dominant that they manage to hide my true self under their wings.

All of my life's complications spring from, or are associated with, these instruments, inner and outer. I live my life looking at the body and mind as if they are me. That's my identity now. I am a human being. All problems are tied to the body or the mind. Even the problems of the world become *my* problems only to the extent they affect either my body or my mind. When I'm not aware of my body and mind, as in deep sleep, my problems seem to disappear, only to magically resurface when I wake up. Moreover, the problems keep mushrooming; they never seem to end. Death might seem to be a way out, alas it isn't, because death simply means my present body is replaced by another equally troublesome body.

Through discernment I realize that the only way to get out of this hopeless situation is to permanently discard my problematic identities. I need to look carefully and learn. When I look outside, I see the world but I don't see myself. I do see my body and I can feel my mind. But they are not the real me either. Since the outside is not too helpful, I need to look within—deep inside, beyond my thoughts and emotions. That is the only way now to discover myself and to reclaim my original identity. The intense desire to be my true self—pure and perfect, eternal and free—and to fling away all of my false identities is known as "longing for freedom" (*mumukṣutva*).

Propelled by such longing, when people practice discernment, non-attachment and the "six treasures," they are able to regain their true identity and become free. What powers their practice is their longing. We see therefore how essential longing is and we know that it works! Sri Ramakrishna's word for intense longing was *vyākulatā.*[1]

How does the longing for spiritual freedom manifest in our life? In several different ways, but also with different degrees of intensity. There is the *mild* form of longing which manifests occasionally but also subsides quickly. It is the kind of longing that makes people visit places of worship now and then, celebrate a few festivals, and even do some basic rituals on special occasions. This sort of longing doesn't last long. It brings a little satisfaction, perhaps eliminates some guilt, but people return to being their usual secular selves without any real inner transformation.

On the other extreme is the *intense* form of longing, whose level of intensity has been compared to a person's desperate rush toward water when one's head is on fire (*Vedānta-sāra,* 30). Or we can compare it to a suffocating person's struggle to breathe. Sri Ramakrishna narrated this story:

> One feels restless for God when one's soul longs for his vision. The guru said to the disciple, "Come with me. I

> shall show you what kind of longing will enable you to see God." Saying this, he took the disciple to a pond and pressed his head under the water. After a few moments he released the disciple and asked, "How did you feel?" The disciple answered: "Oh, I felt as if I were dying! I was longing for a breath of air." (Gospel, 497)

That's the kind of intense longing we need for success in spiritual life. Only when we are really thirsty will we leave no stone unturned to quench our thirst. Listen to these strong words of Swami Vivekananda:

> Until you have that thirst, that desire, you cannot get religion, however you may struggle with your intellect, or your books, or your forms. Until that thirst is awakened in you, you are no better than any atheist; only the atheist is sincere, and you are not. (CW 2. 44-45)

Most of us do have the thirst but probably not enough of it. We lie somewhere on the scale that connects the mild to the intense forms of longing. We slide toward *mild* longing, perhaps even toward *no* longing, when we are not mindful and allow nature to manage the course of our life. But when we live purposefully, with discernment and care, then the intensity of our longing increases. The more intense it gets, the more we realize the urgency of our quest. There is no time to be lost and no effort to be wasted. Then, so to speak, we begin firing on all cylinders.

The intensity in longing for freedom assumes a measure of impatience to be free. How do we level that with the frequent advice we are given to be patient in life? How can patience and impatience coexist? For a spiritual seeker it means to be patient with people and things in the world but impatient about one's spiritual progress. These two can and should coexist. There are forces in the world over which we have little control. All that any of us can do is to try our best and let things take their own course, watching the outcome with patience, because there really is no alternative other than feeling upset or frustrated when things don't turn out the way we want them to. But the impatience with our present progress in spiritual life is what propels us to strive harder.

How can longing be "practiced"? What are the things I need to do? First, I need to remain alert about the nature and extent of my present bondage. I have got to remind myself as often as possible that my bondage is not going disappear on its own. Secondly, I need to always keep the hour of death before my mind, knowing that it can come anytime and making sure that my priorities are right. Finally, I need to intensify my efforts, be it through prayer, *japa,* meditation, study or selfless service, which will help loosen the bonds that tie me to my egocentric existence and connect me to my true nature—which is what will bring me the real freedom that I seek.

Whatever the mind wants, or needs, or is hungry for, that is where the mind settles. If I am hungry for food, the mind thinks of food and settles there until I have food. In the same way, if I am hungry for God, the mind will think of God and settle there—that is how meditation occurs. If I am hungry for spiritual freedom, that is all that the mind will think of and settle there until I become free.

Sooner or later, we all get what we long for. Wisdom lies in longing for the right thing and getting it in the right way.

CHAPTER 13

understanding yoga

The preceding chapters took a close look at each of the Four Basic Practices. Reading about these core practices does improve our understanding, but these practices are meant to be "practiced," not simply to be "studied." When we go ahead and begin the practice, what form does our practice take? It has a name which today has global recognition—yoga.

Yoga is what happens when the Four Basic Practices are put to work. For Vedānta students, yoga as a spiritual discipline is nothing but Four Basic Practices in action.

The popularity of yoga and its inevitable commodification have skewed yoga's original meaning and intent. Yoga, in the truest sense of the term, is a discipline that goes far beyond the physical stretching that promises good health and the rhythmic breathing that promises mental well-being. Yoga has its sights trained on something much higher and much deeper, namely, the divine presence which is beyond both the body and the mind.

Yoga is a word derived from two distinct Sanskrit roots, *yuj* and *yujir*. When traced from *yuj*, yoga means "concentration," and it is primarily in that sense that the word is used in Patañjali's *Yoga-sūtra*. When traced from *yujir*, yoga means "union" or "joining," and that is how Vedānta texts understand it. The two meanings of yoga are related. Yoga as concentration is essentially a means to the goal, while yoga as union is the goal itself. In what sense is "union" the goal? From whom are we separated, which makes union necessary? In short, what *is* the problem that yoga solves?

At the root of the problem is our current experience of being imperfect beings in an imperfect world. All religions agree that our present state is a kind of degeneration. We are told that in some unspecified past everything was perfect, but something bad happened and our natural state of perfection was lost. The religious quest is all about regaining our inherent purity and perfection. This belief is conveyed across traditions through stories and myths which describe our alienation from God and teach us how to go back to God. The biblical story of Adam and Eve's expulsion from the Garden of Eden is one such instance that narrates what led to the separation of human beings from God. Similar stories with interesting variations exist all over the world.

Vedānta's story is not so much about our separation from God (although it can be read that way) but about our separation from our own true self. We are told that in the beginning the Self alone existed through eternity. There was nothing else and no one else. Then something mysterious seems to have happened. A veil of darkness came over (the way it comes over us when we glide into sleep) and resulted in self-forgetfulness.

When the Self's infinitude is forgotten, it begins to think of itself as finite. When its timelessness is forgotten, it views itself as mortal. Constrained in the domain of space and time, the Self now feels neither free nor immortal. The one and only Self, now apparently asleep, projects a dream world filled with many creatures and identifies with one of them as "me" (the way we all do when we sleep and dream). We don't know *when* and we don't know *how,* but it feels as if the Self, divine in nature, went to sleep and became a human being in the dream. That is the person you and I see every time we stand before a mirror. I am the infinite being who is asleep and dreaming that I am finite. In my dream I am no longer the real me. I have become separated from my true self.

The implications of this separation are cataclysmic, something every one of us experiences every day of our lives. The veil of ignorance produces my sense of incompleteness, which results in the rise of desire. To fulfill the desire, I need to work, which leads to the experience of joy or sorrow depending on whether or not my desire is fulfilled. The desires are many and multifarious, so are the actions and their results. Whether I realize it or not, the truth is that I am being hustled along in the vicious cycle (called *saṁsāra*) of repeated births and deaths with its never-ending stream of karma and its results.

The chain reaction is not difficult to understand: Ignorance ⇝ Desire ⇝ Action, which produces results and leads to repeated rebirths.

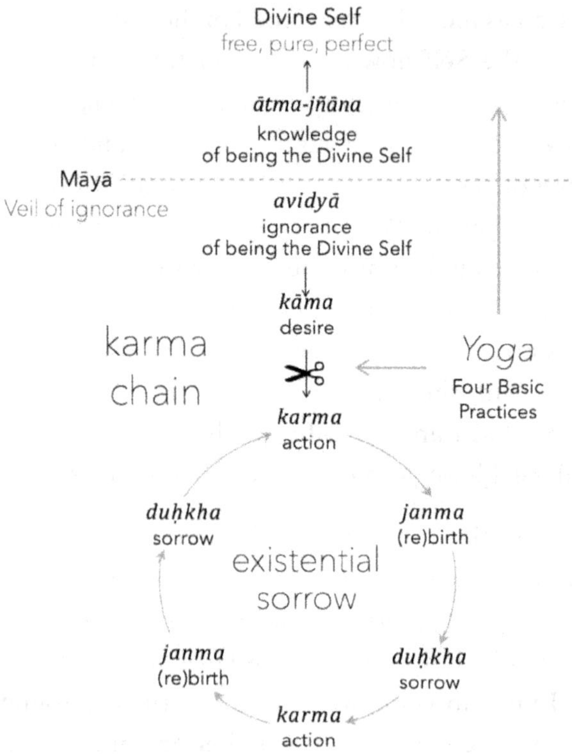

The chain is unforgiving and relentless, it is strong and almost unbreakable. The weakest link in the chain, and the only breakable one, is one that connects desire with karma. This is where yoga—the form that the Four Basic Practices take—steps in. Yoga snaps the link that connects desire with karma, effectively breaking the chain and ending the dream. Only then does my veil of ignorance disappear and I discover that I am no longer the finite self that I thought I was. I wake up and find to my great joy that I am divine and have always been infinite and immortal.

Since the Four Basic Practices can take various forms when put into practice, yoga can manifest in many different flavors. It was Swami Vivekananda who first systematized our understanding of yoga based on the powers of the mind. The mind has three major powers—the power to *think,* the power to *feel,* and the power to *strive*. The power to think employs reasoning. The power to feel employs emotions. The power to strive employs the will. While these powers—to *know*, to *feel*, and to *strive*—are present in all, everyone may not have each of these developed in equal measure. Usually one of the powers dominates and the other two play a supporting role.

The dominant tendency in some people is to apply reasoning and logic to everything. They do have feelings and will power, but these play a supporting role in the Four Basic Practices of these people, giving their practices a specific color and form—and these are usually thought of as belonging to Jñāna Yoga. Similarly, the Four Basic Practices of those who are especially sensitive to emotions and feelings take on a color and form that is thought of as Bhakti Yoga. The Four Basic Practices of those who prioritize their will-power internally to control and discipline the mind take the form of Rāja Yoga.

When it is done externally to improve the quality and efficiency of work, the Four Basic Practices take the form of Karma Yoga.

The four yogas are thus powered by the three functions of the mind, and—not surprisingly—each of the four yogas is led by one of the Four Basic Practices. When the predominant practice is discernment and the other three practices play a supporting role, the result is Jñāna Yoga. In the same way, when the dominant practice is non-attachment, the result is Karma Yoga. When the "six treasures" are dominant in a person's practice, the result is Rāja Yoga. When the intense longing is dominant, the resulting practice takes the form of Bhakti Yoga. Each of the Four Basic Practices becomes the primary tool that snaps the link which connects desire with karma. Once the link is broken, the relative world disappears and the Divine is revealed.

It was Swami Vivekananda's ingenious insight to classify all spiritual disciplines into four categories, each of which is a "yoga," a way to join the finite with the Infinite, a way to unite the creature with the Creator, or a way to experience the oneness that undergirds everything that exists. What distinguishes one yoga from another is not the different practices, but the *same* practice done with a mind that has a *different* dominant characteristic. Vivekananda did not invent the names Jñāna Yoga, Bhakti Yoga, Rāja Yoga, and Karma Yoga, but he invested them with a new meaning. They represent the different forms the Four Basic Practices take when placed in real life situations by people with different mindsets. As we have seen, yoga is what happens when the Four Basic Practices are put into practice. For a clear understanding of this, there is no better source than Swami Vivekananda's insightful and inspiring books on the four yogas.

How long does the practice have to continue before spiritual freedom is attained? There are said to be three steps to freedom—and we now turn to those in the next chapter.

CHAPTER 14

steps to freedom

What makes me do the Four Basic Practices is my longing to be free. The journey from bondage to spiritual freedom is said to occur in three steps, but sometimes in only two, in rare cases even one, depending on the fitness of the student. The Four Basic Practices initiate the process of fitness. The more adept I become with the Four Basic Practices, the more fit they make me and the fewer the steps I need in order to be free.

Those who have perfected themselves in the Four Basic Practices belong to the category of the magnificent. They are considered the best (*uttama*) among the students. Those who are still struggling, still failing most of the time, are the mediocre ones, somewhat uncharitably called the lowest (*kaniṣṭha*) among the students. The rest are the middlings, located somewhere in the middle (*madhyama*), failing at times and succeeding at other times but doggedly keeping up the practice.

How many steps I need to reach freedom depends largely on what kind of student I am—mediocre, middling, or magnificent. My status is not carved in stone. If I am mediocre at present, it doesn't mean that is how I'll remain forever. I can improve and raise myself to be among the magnificent if I continue undeterred with the Four Basic Practices with dedication, determination and perseverance.

So what are these steps to freedom?

Step 1: "Hearing" *(śravaṇa)*

The first step is to know the truth—the truth of my present bondage and the way to get out of it. In ancient times this literally occurred through hearing. There were no books then and the student had to go to a teacher and hear the teachings. Hearing remains a key method how we learn even today. When we read books, in our mind we "hear" the words on the paper. We are now also used to getting knowledge through lectures and conversations, audiobooks and podcasts. When we think about what we have heard, we also hear ourselves and often have extended conversations with ourselves.

Hearing is an art. It requires discernment. If we give the same attention to every sound around us, it may be fun for a while, but soon enough we'll get tired or bored if we don't also go crazy. We instinctively tune out some of the sounds in order to focus on what really matters. Sometimes we cannot do it well. While chanting a mantra, for instance, we are expected to filter out all sounds except the sound of the mantra. Distracted by our own inner chatter, we often fail to do so, effectively killing the *japa* practice. When we listen to the words of the teacher, or of a scripture, we are expected to hear only that, and nothing else. It is no easy matter, but that's why even hearing needs to be practiced well.

There is one other thing that we need to know—and that is about access. Only those who are very close to the family are granted access to every part of one's home. Others may come only up to the room where guests are received. Likewise in the matter of hearing, only that which is really vital to me should be given access to the deepest core of my being. All other sounds deserve only limited access, so I can deal with them appropriately and get them out of my mind when they are no longer needed. The words of the scripture and the teacher are a different story. They need to be granted total access. Those precious words are to be taken in, deep inside us, to be pondered over in the sacred silence of the heart.

The knowledge received from the teacher is of two types —one is related to *doing,* and the other is related to *being.* The instruction regarding *doing* generally begins with teaching the student how to pray. Traditionally, the first prayer taught to the student is the Gāyatrī, a powerful prayer to awaken one's latent power of spiritual intuition. But there are other prayers as well, either spontaneous, self-composed or from existing texts. Doing mantra *japa* is also an act of prayer. When done with heartfelt sincerity and devotion, prayer combines in it all the elements of the Four Basic Practices. It is prayer that cleanses the heart and makes it ready to receive the teaching.

The teacher's instructions regarding *being* primarily point to the student's true identity. Who I really am is described in different ways. Theistically, my true nature takes the form of a relationship with the Divine. In personal terms, God is my eternal father or mother, and I am God's child. I may also see God as my master, my friend, or my beloved. With a heart filled with parental love, it is possible to see God even as my child. There is no limit to the ways in which I can relate to God.

In most cases, bonding is established not with "God" in a generic sense, but more specifically with the Divine associated with a name and a form. In Sanskrit, this favored form through which the Divine becomes accessible is called *iṣṭa-devatā*. The journey is often described as one from the tangible to the intangible—from form to beyond form, from name to beyond name. It is a practical approach, taking support when we need it and outgrowing the need for it when we are strong and able.

Philosophically, my relationship with God is similar to that between a part and the whole. The intensity of my love and the clarity of my perception keep reducing the distance that separates me from God. As we come closer to each other, a point is reached when God and I are no longer two but one. The relationship reaches its zenith in unity. How amazing that it was the one Being all along who for a while appeared as two! Such is the nondual experience described in the *Bṛhadāraṇyaka Upaniṣad*

(1.4.10): "I am the Infinite One." There cannot be two infinities. Whatever exists is one. The existence of the "many" may well be a myth.

The teacher's instruction (as in *Taittirīya Upaniṣad,* 2.1.3) may be as simple as pointing out the ultimate Being to be "real, conscious and infinite." Perhaps the teacher may also instruct the student to do a simple experiment, such as placing a pinch of salt in a glass of water. The next day —we read in the *Chāndogya Upaniṣad* (6.13.1-3)—the student is asked to bring the salt which was placed in the water. It is naturally dissolved by then, so the salt is not visible. The teacher tells the student to sip the water from the top, from the middle, and from the bottom of the glass. Finding the water salty throughout, the student says that, although not visible, the salt is present everywhere in the water. The teacher then points out that, exactly in the same way, although not visible, Being not only is present everywhere but is also the self of everything that exists.

तत् सत्यं, स आत्मा, तत् त्वं असि ।

Tat satyaṁ, sa ātmā, tat tvaṁ asi.

That is the truth. That is the self. You are that.

Hearing these words, the student is expected to look within and find out who exactly "that" is. Discovering "that" and its relation to "me" is the crux of spiritual life. How long the discovery will take is directly related to how fit the student is. When the right answer flashes in the heart, the student encounters the ineffable Being who is both "transcendent and immanent." This life-changing experience "cuts asunder the knots of the heart, dispels all doubts, and destroys all karmas" (Muṇḍaka Upaniṣad, 2.2.8).

All of this happens immediately as soon as the teaching is heard in the case of those who are perfected in the Four Basic Practices. Merely hearing the teacher express the truth is enough for these magnificent students to wake up from the sleep of ignorance into the light of the Infinite. Blessed are those who are free and blessed is the moment they wake up! Such occasions are special and sacred but also rare, and such students are also extremely rare.

For everyone else, the hearing of the teaching leads not to spiritual freedom but to doubts and questions. That makes it necessary to move to step 2.

Step 2: "Reflection" (*manana*)

Hearing the teacher's instructions and pondering over them, the student's reservations regarding the scripture, which is a means of knowledge (*pramāṇa*), are generally removed. Can I trust what the scriptures say? What is the best way to study and understand a scripture? How can the wisdom in the scripture become my own?—questions such as these are answered through the teacher's instructions. But what persist for most students are doubts regarding the object of knowledge (*prameya*), in other words, who God is—philosophically, what the nature of "that" (*tat*) is and how it is related to "me" (*aham*).

When I receive a valuable equipment as gift, I may recognize that it is precious but remain unsure about how to operate it or how to take care of it. I'll likely bring it home and examine it carefully, study it from every angle, in order to learn more about it. That is what happens to us after hearing the teaching. We recognize that it is important but we are not able to fully understand it because of doubts and questions. The teacher's instructions need to be "brought home," that is, inside my mind and heart, so I can examine them with care to solve the doubts that are still lingering in my mind. To do this effectively, I need to intensify my Four Basic Practices to gain greater understanding.

What does God being my father or mother mean? How is this relationship similar to or different from my relationship with my biological parents? How can I be God's child without ever having seen or known God? In the supreme intensity of love, can any distance remain between God and me? Maybe there is just Being (*sat*) manifesting apparently as two, God (*īśvara*) and the embodied soul (*jīva*)? But how can the infinite perfection of the Divine be identical with the little mortal human that I am?—questions similar to these arise and the student tries to grapple with them. These questions are related to the seeming impossibility (*asambhāvanā*) of a relationship with the Divine.

Remembering the words of the teacher and diving deep into the texts, the student begins to reflect. Like hearing, reflecting is also an art. Doing it haphazardly yields only haphazard results. Reflecting must be done in a disciplined way.

The most important thing in the practice of reflection is steadiness, that is, the ability to hold and keep an idea or a thought in the forefront of the mind in order to examine it minutely from every angle. This becomes a challenge if the mind is habituated to flitting from one thought to another. Acquiring the ability to stabilize the mind and focusing it for a length of time on a given idea is a must for a successful practice of reflection.

All the means of knowledge—such as direct perception, scripture, inference—can be summoned to help in the process of examining an idea and assessing its worth. It is like solving a crossword puzzle. Getting one or two words right makes it progressively easier to find the other words. In exactly the same way, one insight leads to another and the initial doubts begin to disappear. What did not make sense earlier now begins to look like the only sensible answer. Doubts are replaced by clarity. Questions melt away.

For most middling students, the practice of reflection can take days or months, even years—depending on where they stand on the scale that separates the mediocre from the magnificent. But eventually all obstacles vanish when their doubts are resolved and they attain spiritual freedom.

But that may not happen in every case. It is possible to resolve my doubts regarding the nature of my relationship with God—and find that I am still tied to my body and mind, still stuck to my mortal human identity, still enmeshed in the web of ideas and concepts, and nowhere near experiencing the spiritual freedom that I seek. The reason is that another obstacle, a more formidable one, is blocking my path. This cannot be overcome merely through reflection.

That takes me to the next step.

Step 3: "Meditation" (*nididhyāsana*)

The deadly obstruction that survives reflection is known as "contrary experience" (*viparīta-bhāvanā*). Deep reflection gives us the joy of intellectual conviction but we also see its limitations. Even when I understand how connected I am with God, my daily life continues to contradict my conviction. I still feel that I am mortal, unable to experience my connection with the divine, hopelessly locked up in my body-mind identity. My present human persona feels real even if not entirely satisfactory. In comparison, my relationship with God feels like a mere hope or an intellectual formulation or only a belief. It lacks the force of reality.

The humbling truth is that most of us belong to the mediocre category of students. Our aspirations are high and our intentions are noble, but something subtle and sinister is blocking our path. A distorted self-perception and wrong habits of thinking acquired over many lifetimes cannot be wished away easily. The only way to remove this seemingly impregnable obstacle is to pursue the Four Basic Practices with even greater intensity. At this stage, it is difficult to move ahead without total commitment and self-discipline. Deep faith in the teacher, a refined mind, and study of scriptures are great assets—and yet the deepest core of my being may still be clouded, still vulnerable to the pull of the material world.

What is needed now is to keep reflecting, but to also move beyond reflection and strive to encounter the truth in the deepest core of my being. All the thought forms (*vṛtti*) in the mind must cease except one—who I am in relation to God. Meditation is a search, a continuous search, a kind of inner wandering (*parivrajana*) in search of the truth that resides within. The practice of reflection needs the support of ideas and concepts. Meditation is a step beyond, no longer engaging with concepts but with the truth they point to. It is time to move the gaze from the finger pointing to the moon and to look directly at the moon itself.

Leaving ideas behind is far from easy. Encountering reality unfiltered by concepts is no joke. Any headway in meditation can occur only through divine grace and deep faith in oneself and in the truth. The two steps of hearing and reflection are expected to have eliminated many of the distractions on the path. The third step is meant to overcome our perennial clinging to the body-mind-centered "I" and to push us toward *being* the real self in search of its true home. There is no knowing how long the search will last. There is no knowing how it will end.

The thought of "time" is a distraction. The thought of "results" is another distraction. In meditation both have to be left behind. Just holding on to one's self and allowing grace to guide the search is all that is needed.

What passes for meditation usually has a beginning and an end, and is often practiced more than once a day. But meditation as *nididhyāsana* is different. It shows us that meditation doesn't—*shouldn't*—end when we get up from the meditation seat. We are expected to maintain the awareness of a specific relationship with God not only when we are praying and meditating but even when we are doing "other things." No matter what I'm doing at present, I don't stop being human and never forget that I am human. In precisely the same way, in the practice of *nididhyāsana,* no matter what I do, I shouldn't stop being in relationship with God and constantly remain aware of that relationship. Meditation as *nididhyāsana* is less about *doing* and more about *being*. Doing is bound by time, being is timeless.

Living all the time with full awareness of the self in search of God is tough. This requires enormous faith, resilience, courage. It is not a task for the weak. It calls for unusual inner strength, purity and discipline. It is possible in time to taste success in bits and pieces if I patiently practice *nididhyāsana* with dogged determination and with a mind that is uncluttered by distractions. There will be many failures along the way, but if I persevere undeterred in the practice, intervals of forgetfulness become progressively shorter, moments of encountering the truth become longer and sharper.

Although the three steps to freedom have a chronological feel, in practice they often occur concurrently. It is neither easy nor necessary to know when one step ends and when it's time to take the next one. After the initial hearing process and the rise of doubts and questions, reflection naturally follows. As things begin to get sorted out, meditation is the inevitable next step to dive deeper into myself. Over time and with sustained practice, the hearing, the reflection and meditation keep getting better, removing my initial doubts, edging me toward perfection, and filling my being with increasing clarity.

Like everything in life, the search will end one day. It could be tomorrow, perhaps even today—or it could take years. There is no knowing when grace will switch the light on. But it *will* happen provided I don't slacken my efforts or give up the quest. That is when I will stand face to face with truth. Which is really a ridiculous way to express it. For at that point, words fail. How can we express the inexpressible? There is no way to describe the experience except to say that, whatever it is that happens, it ends all suffering for ever. All that remains is the awareness of supreme bliss. I remain immersed in bliss but without the idea of "I," since there is nothing else and no one else from whom I am separate. All that exists is existence itself. *Being* that existence, forever free from the constraints of *becoming* someone—*that* is freedom in the truest sense of the term.

The Four Basic Practices are the backbone of the steps to freedom. The more refined our practices become, the closer we get to the goal of supreme freedom.

CHAPTER 15

from doing to being

The Four Basic Practices remain with me from beginning to end—they determine my fitness to start the spiritual journey, they support me through my struggles, they stay with me until I attain freedom. They become my friends, my protectors, my guides. How long the struggle will be, what ups and downs I'll encounter, how I'll face the challenges along the way—all of these things are determined by the quality of my Four Basic Practices. Spiritual life is nothing but a continual effort to improve the quality of my practice. The more proficient I become in the Four Basic Practices, the quicker is my progress.

Yoga is what happens naturally when we start practicing the Four Basic Practices. But there is no need to agonize over which yoga I should practice or which yoga is right for me. I am better off simply trying to do the Four Basic Practices as best I can in a way that comes naturally to me. Whatever forms my practices take—and whichever yoga-label is attached to them—what I should be mindful about is that I am earnest, ready to put in the hard work, and willing to learn from my mistakes. The real value in spiritual life is the inner transformation it can bring about in me. Is my life being regularly updated and upgraded like a good software? Am I becoming a better version of myself day after day? Am I serious about eliminating my weaknesses? Am I getting closer to God? —this is what matters. Everything else is a waste of time and energy.

When I continue the practice with faith and dedication, patience and perseverance, results are bound to come. My spiritual fitness increases, the practice deepens, and I can feel a certain lightness of being. For a long time the Four Basic Practices may have been what I *did,* but they have the power to change now to who I *am.* If I must look for miracles, then the transformation from doing to being is certainly one that deserves attention. Although breathing is an activity every one of us is engaged in from the moment we are born, it is not what we think of as something we have to do. Most of the time we just do it without even being aware that we are doing it. It is so much a part of us that we simply *are* creatures who breathe, not creatures who have to *do* breathing. We want the same thing to happen to each of the Four Basic Practices.

The transformation from doing to being is a common feature in the pursuit of any art. When I begin learning to play a musical instrument, I have to be mindful of every little detail and do everything very methodically. Most of my attention is on the process and the effort to do everything correctly. After much practice, when the muscle memory is built, I am able to do things without any effort, almost instinctively. It is only then that I become free to express myself fully and unreservedly. The best musical pieces don't emerge when a musician is "making" music. The outstanding pieces are born when the musician's ego gets out of the way and creativity flows unobstructed. Doing is relatively easy, what is tough is simply being.

Living spiritually is one of the most refined arts of all time. In the beginning, there is a lot of doing—books to read, thoughts to think, and things to do. There is a lot to be mindful about, such as my thoughts, my words, my actions and reactions, my relationships, my attitudes. All of this can be daunting and intimidating. What keeps me on track is faith in myself and in my ideal, my determination to never give up, the awareness that there is a higher power at work, and the never-failing hope that grace will descend any moment—and it indeed does when I patiently persevere with the practice. When that happens, there is a clear shift from doing to being.

I may discover one day that I no longer need to practice discernment, because it has become my default state of being. Every thought I think, every word I speak, every action I do is effortlessly funneled through discernment. There is no longer any need to practice non-attachment, because it has become so much a part of my nature that I cannot get trapped in attachments even if I tried. The mind and the senses become restrained on their own, withdrawing spontaneously when needed, the way a tortoise retracts in its shell (Gita, 2. 58). If the mind and the senses do manage to break free on a rare occasion, something within is able to pull them back quickly. I may stop shuddering when faced with difficult dilemmas, unsolvable situations, or nasty people; forbearance becomes my second nature, infusing all pain with a meaning that neutralizes suffering. The mind becomes so disciplined that, wherever it is directed, it is able to achieve concentration with ease. Deep faith fills my entire being and becomes the measure of who I really am (Gita 17. 3). Intense longing for freedom never really leaves the heart even when I am engaged in my daily activities. How amazing it will be when all of this happens to me!

A story from Buddha's life comes to mind. As his teachings spread and monasteries sprung up everywhere in the Indian subcontinent, rules were created to train the novices. Buddha continued to abide by those rules to the last detail even with a frail body in his old age. His immediate disciples said to him, "Venerable Teacher, you made these rules to instill discipline in the young monks. You don't need to follow these rules since you are already enlightened." Hearing this, Buddha smiled and told his disciples, "When I was young, I observed all of these rules for years. They have become an inseparable part of my life. I no longer follow them. It is they who follow me." That is exactly what happens when doing is transformed into being.

When I move from doing to being, I don't need to *do* the practices because they have become who I *am*. Just as breathing happens on its own, my Four Basic Practices get done on their own. That is the sign that I am close to perfection. The bridge from mediocrity to magnificence is crossed. The Four Basic Practices take me to the threshold that separates the relative from the absolute.

What should I do after that? Nothing beyond "hearing" the teaching and turning my gaze toward the east. The sun is already rising above the horizon and there is Light —inside, outside, everywhere.

Finally I am awake. I am free.

I am home.

notes

1. RECALIBRATING VEDĀNTA

1. 'The idea is that the Vedas were never written; the idea is, they never came into existence. I was told once by a Christian missionary that their scriptures have a historical character, and therefore are true, to which I replied, 'Mine have no historical character and *therefore* they are true; yours being historical, they were evidently made by some man the other day. Yours are man-made and mine are not; their non-historicity is in their favor.'" (CW, 3. 334)
2. "The Upanishads do not reveal the life of any teacher, but simply teach principles. They are [as it were] shorthand notes taken down of discussion in [learned assemblies], generally in the courts of kings. ... Those of you who may have studied some of the Upanishads can understand how they are condensed shorthand sketches. After long discussions had been held, they were taken down, possibly from memory. The difficulty is that you get very little of the background." (CW, 1. 446)
3. A case in point is the way Sri Ramakrishna's spiritual practices became classified in many of his biographies, which refer to his practice of Vaiṣṇava and Tantra under the guidance of Jaṭādhāri and the Bhairavī Brāhmaṇī, practice of Vedānta under Totā Puri, besides his practice of Islam and Christianity.
4. "It is very hard to find any common name for our religion, seeing that this religion is a collection, so to speak, of various religions, of various ideas, of various ceremonials and forms, all gathered together almost without a name, and without a church, and without an organization. The only point where, perhaps, all our sects agree is that we all believe in the scriptures—the Vedas. This perhaps is certain that no man can have a right to be called Hindu who does not admit the supreme authority of the Vedas." (CW, 3. 228)

2. SPIRITUAL FITNESS

1. See the Gītā (4. 34): "Know the Truth by prostrating, by asking questions, and by serving. Those who have realized the Truth will instruct you in that knowledge."
2. "Freedom is the only condition of growth; take that off, the result is degeneration." (CW 5. 23)
3. *Reminiscences of Swami Vivekananda* (Kolkata: Advaita Ashrama), 196. For an inspiring account of Sister Christine's life, please read Pravrajika Vrajaprana, *A Portrait of Sister Christine* (Kolkata: Advaita Ashrama).

6. RESTRAINING THE MIND

1. For a helpful discussion of the *yamas* and *niyamas*, see Pravrajika Vrajaprana, *Vedānta: The Next Steps* (Vedānta Press, 2025), 91-149.

7. RESTRAINING THE SENSES

1. See also Swamiji's lecture on "Sankhya and Vedānta (CW, 2. 458): "I see a blackboard. How does the knowledge come? What the German philosophers call 'the thing-in-itself' of the blackboard is unknown, I can never know it. Let us call it *x*. The blackboard *x* acts on my mind, and the mind reacts. The mind is like a lake. Throw a stone in a lake and a reactionary wave comes towards the stone; this wave is not like the stone at all, it is a wave. The blackboard *x* is like a stone which strikes the mind and the mind throws up a wave towards it, and this wave is what we call the black-board.

   "I see you. You as reality are unknown and unknowable. You are *x* and you act upon my mind, and the mind throws a wave in the direction from which the impact comes, and that wave is what I call Mr. or Mrs. So-and-so.

   "There are two elements in the perception, one coming from outside and the other from inside, and the combination of these two, *x* + mind, is our external universe. All knowledge is by reaction."

9. FORBEARANCE

1. See also (CW, I. 38-39): "This is a great lesson for us all to learn, that in all matters the two extremes are alike. The extreme positive and the extreme negative are always similar. When the vibrations of light are too slow, we do not see them, nor do we see them when they are too rapid. So with sound; when very low in pitch, we do not hear it; when very high, we do not hear it either. Of like nature is the difference between resistance and non-resistance. One man does not resist because he is weak, lazy, and cannot, not because he will not; the other man knows that he can strike an irresistible blow if he likes; yet he not only does not strike, but blesses his enemies. The one who from weakness resists not commits a sin, and as such cannot receive any benefit from the non-resistance; while the other would commit a sin by offering resistance. Buddha gave up his throne and renounced his position, that was true renunciation; but there cannot be any question of renunciation in the case of a beggar who has nothing to renounce.

   "So we must always be careful about what we really mean when we speak of this non-resistance and ideal love. We must first take care to understand whether we have the power of resistance or not. Then, having the power, if we renounce it and do not resist, we are doing a grand act of love; but if we cannot resist, and yet, at the same time, try to deceive ourselves into the belief that we are actuated by motives of the highest love, we are doing the exact opposite."

10. CONCENTRATION

1. "How has all the knowledge in the world been gained but by the concentration of the powers of the mind? The world is ready to give up its secrets if we only know how to knock, how to give it the necessary blow. The strength and force of the blow come through concentration. There is no limit to the power of the human mind. The more concentrated it is, the more power is brought to bear on one point; that is the secret." CW, I. 130-31.

   "We have but one method of acquiring knowledge. From the lowest man to the highest Yogi, all have to use the same method; and that method is what is called concentration. The chemist who works in his laboratory concentrates all the powers of his mind, brings them into one focus, and throws them on the elements; and the elements stand analyzed, and thus his knowledge comes. The astronomer has also concentrated the powers of his mind and brought them into one focus; and he throws them on to objects through his telescope; and stars and systems roll forward and give up their secrets to him. So it is in every case—with the professor in his chair, the student with his book—with every man who is working to know.

"You are hearing me, and if my words interest you, your mind will become concentrated on them; and then suppose a clock strikes, you will not hear it, on account of this concentration; and the more you are able to concentrate your mind, the better you will understand me; and the more I concentrate my love and powers, the better I shall be able to give expression to what I want to convey to you. The more this power of concentration, the more knowledge is acquired, because this is the one and only method of acquiring knowledge.

"Even the lowest shoeblack, if he gives more concentration, will black shoes better; the cook with concentration will cook a meal all the better. In making money, or in worshipping God, or in doing anything, the stronger the power of concentration, the better will that thing be done. This is the one call, the one knock, which opens the gates of nature, and lets out floods of light. This, the power of concentration, is the only key to the treasure-house of knowledge." CW, 2. 390-91.

2. "The ideal of the Yogi, the whole science of Yoga, is directed to the end of teaching men how, by intensifying the power of assimilation, to shorten the time for reaching perfection, instead of slowly advancing from point to point and waiting until the whole human race has become perfect. All the great prophets, saints, and seers of the world—what did they do? In one span of life they lived the whole life of humanity, traversed the whole length of time that it takes ordinary humanity to come to perfection. In one life they perfect themselves; they have no thought for anything else, never live a moment for any other idea, and thus the way is shortened for them. This is what is meant by concentration, intensifying the power of assimilation, thus shortening the time. Raja-Yoga is the science which teaches us how to gain the power of concentration." CW, 1. 157.

12. LONGING FOR FREEDOM

1. In Sri Ramakrishna's biographies we read about how intense his longing was to see the Divine Mother and to personally ascertain whether she was for real. It is a humbling experience to look at our own longing for God and realize how woefully feeble it is!

index

about the author

A monk of the Ramakrishna Order since 1976, Swami Tyagananda is the head of Ramakrishna Vedanta Society, Boston, and Hindu Chaplain at Harvard and MIT. He has written, edited and translated fifteen books.

facebook.com/VedantaBoston

also by swami tyagananda

Books

Knowing the Knower: A Jnana Yoga Manual

Walking the Walk: A Karma Yoga Manual

Looking Deeply: Vivekacūḍāmaṇi

A Drop of Nectar: Amritabindu Upanishad

Audio

Insights from the Gita

Kathopanishad

Narada Bhakti Suta

Vivekacūḍāmaṇi

www.ingramcontent.com/pod-product-compliance
Lightning Source LLC
Chambersburg PA
CBHW060257050426
42448CB00009B/1672
* 9 7 8 0 9 9 8 7 3 1 4 6 9 *